Jumping Sp

Jumping Spider Pet Owners Guide.

By

Edward Dunbarn

Table of Contents

Introduction

Jumping Spiders are part of the Salticidae family, which is the largest family of spiders consisting of approximately 6080 known species and 635 genera. This family accounts for around 10% of the whole spider population.

Although most common in tropical areas, Jumping Spiders can actually be found in nearly every type of habitat in the world, apart from the extreme polar regions.

In most recent years, they have become a popular domestic pet for those who like to keep more exotic and unusual creatures.

Chapter 1: The Jumping Spider

Like all other spiders, the Jumping Spider has eight legs. Its body is compact and usually looks square with relatively short legs. It will often be covered in dense hairs or scales that can be brightly coloured. This body hair helps them grip when climbing.

Life Span
These creatures don't have very long life spans, even with the most perfect care and although some have been known to live to around two to three years old the average life span for one kept as a pet is six months to a year.

Interesting Features
Size
These spiders are pretty tiny in comparison to other spider species and on average their body length ranges from 1 to 25mm (0.04 – 0.98 inches). As a size comparison, some of these spiders are no bigger than a human's thumb nail.

Colours
Jumping spiders are found in a variety of colours and patterns depending on which type it is; they can be black, grey, brown or tan with gray, yellow, blue, red, white or green markings. The many different colours make these creatures all the more attractive and interesting.

Some Jumping Spiders will mimic other creatures, for example, the Rhene Flavicomans is also known as the Wasp Mimic Jumping Spider because it has black and yellow markings like, you guessed it, a wasp.

Eyes

These creatures have their eyes in an odd arrangement with two large eyes at the front in the centre of their 'head' and two pairs of smaller eyes which can either be located on either side of the large eyes or can even be found on the top of the spider's 'head; depending on the type of Jumping Spider it is.

The two large front eyes work in a similar way to a telescope; their lenses are immobile with a long, liquid filled tube extending down from the eyes. This liquid – scientists aren't exactly sure what it is - acts as a second lens and causes the light to bend so the eyes collect and focus the light and the liquid spreads it out, thus enabling these spiders to see their surroundings in a huge amount of detail despite their tiny size.

Another thing that makes their eyes so special is that the retinas can swivel on their own, giving the spider the ability to look around without physically having to move its head, which makes it a great hunter. As well as being able to see in great detail, scientists also believe that these spiders see in full colour, which is unusual for arachnids.

Legs

Their front legs are usually thicker and longer than their other legs and many people believe this is why they can jump so well but in actual fact they use their back legs more and the front ones tend to be used mainly for support and to 'dance' in their mating rituals.

As their name suggests, the Jumping Spider is an amazing jumper. You may think that these creatures must have incredibly muscular legs in order for them to jump such large distances but this actually isn't true. Their ability to leap up to fifty times their own body length is down to segmented legs and blood flow. When they are ready to jump they cause an extreme change in their hemolymph pressure (which is the Jumping Spider equivalent of human blood pressure).

By contracting muscles in their upper bodies the spiders can force blood flow to their legs, causing them to extend rapidly. It is this sudden and incredibly quick leg extension that causes them to shoot off in the direction they are aiming for.

Hearing
These spiders don't actually have ears yet can hear very well. This is due to sensory hairs along their bodies taking in sound wave vibrations and sending signals to the spider's brain.

Hunting
Unlike other species of spiders that spin webs in order to catch their food, the Jumping Spider actually hunts its prey. Of course, when you have such a powerful jump as these creatures do, you don't have to sit and wait for your dinner. Instead they stalk and pounce on their prey, using venom to subdue it and make it liquidated so they can suck it up.

To stabilize their landing, they spin a quick line of silk which acts as a drag line when they jump, as well as being a safety net should they need to stop mid-jump.

Chelicerae
These are the appendages in front of the spider's mouth that look like fangs. The venom is injected into prey through these chelicerae. In Jumping Spiders these are often colourful such as an iridescent green or purple, depending on which type of spider it is.

These are very interesting because when handling or taking photographs, the chelicerae often appear to change colour. This is due to the chelicerae colour being both pigmented and a structural coloration which is affected by the viewing or lighting angle. Often, a change in colour is because light has hit the chelicerae at a different angle, causing changes in the structural coloration.

A temporary colour change can occur after a molt when the chelicerae are still soft or sometimes can be caused by certain food sources but this doesn't happen very often.

Another theory that has been put forward, but hasn't been proven, is that the chelicerae colour is dependent on whether the venom gland is full or empty. Therefore, if your spider has just killed prey their chelicerae may look different than before its meal.

Other suggestions are that hydration, fat deposits, hormones or other physiological changes could cause a change in the structural colour, but again more research would need to be done to confirm this.

Common Terms

If you are doing research via the Internet or on forums and social media groups, you may come across some terms that are used quite a lot.

Spiderling or Sling – A baby Jumping Spider

Sac – A Jumping Spider nest. As mentioned earlier, Jumping Spiders don't spin webs but they do have silk which they use to build tiny sacs - or 'hammocks' as some owners refer to them - to sleep or rest in. A female spider will build an egg sac in which to lay her eggs and both male and female will build a sac when molting.

Gravid – This is a term used for a female Jumping Spider that is ready to lay fertile eggs.

Phid – This refers to a Jumping Spider from the Phidippus family; the most common type of Jumping Spider to keep as a pet.

Cephalothorax – This is the scientific name for the 'head' of a Jumping Spider.

Pedipalps – The appendages located at the front of the spider on either side of the chelicerae. They kind of look like an extra pair of short fluffy legs but the males will eventually have a more bulbous look compared to females and will use their pedipalps to transfer sperm to the female when mating.

CB – Captive Bred, meaning a spider that has been born and raised in captivity either as a pet or by a breeder.

WC – Wild Caught meaning a spider that has been captured from the environment.

Families, Genus And Species

It is often quite confusing when you look into Jumping Spiders because you will hear a lot of scientific names as well as common terms.

To clarify, Jumping Spiders all belong to the family of spiders known as Salticidae. As there are so many spiders belonging to this family they have been grouped into genus. For example, the Phidippus is one genus, the Maratus and Saratus are another.

The Peacock Jumping Spider

From either the Maratus or Saratus genus, these Jumping Spiders are colourful and often sought out by those wanting to own an exotic spider. There are lots more of these spiders being discovered and as such some of these species, although under the umbrella term of Peacock Jumping Spider, are as yet unnamed. Unfortunately, they are native to Australia and therefore can only be kept as pets there. Australia have very strict laws with regards to imports and exports and as such it is illegal to send these spiders abroad so you will not be able to purchase one from overseas.

There are no laws that state these cannot be kept as pets however, if you are lucky enough to live in Australia then there is nothing stopping you from finding one in the wild and keeping it. They tend to be found in dry, scrubby habitats.

The downside to keeping them as pets is that these spiders have a very short life span and males only tend to live a year or less.

Peacock Jumping Spiders are incredibly small at around 3-5mm which is approximately twice the size of a flea. This small size means they are very difficult to keep as a pet because it is hard to source food for them.

Many people state that their size makes them very difficult to breed although some have managed to breed successfully over a couple of generations. However, these tend to have been done purely for research purposes. Mostly people will take photographs of these spiders and then release them back out into the wild.

It is worth noting that whilst these spiders are incredibly beautiful with their multi-coloured abdomens and flaps which are raised up like Peacock feathers – hence the name – the males actually only develop this colouring and flaps for the last few months of their lives in order to attract a mate and won't be brightly coloured until their final molt.

Chapter 2: The Jumping Spider As A Pet

Does A Jumping Spider Make A Good Pet?
Yes!

If you like spiders then, in my opinion, these are definitely the cutest variety. Not only that but these spiders are so incredibly fascinating you could spend hours just watching them go about their daily business.

Many people who class themselves as having Arachnophobia – a fear of spiders – claim that these little Jumping Spiders have helped them overcome this fear and that they are not frightened of them at all. Whether this is due to their size or is because close up – with their big eyes and furry faces - they look more like a cuddly cat or friendly dog than a scary bug I don't know but many people who would refuse to keep a Tarantula or a Black Widow in their houses have no problem keeping, feeding and handling these tiny jumpers.

There is no denying that the more colourful ones are incredibly beautiful although even the plainer grey or tan ones are attractive. The Phidippus Audax is black with white spots on it's back which often resemble a heart shape. Depending on the placement of these white markings they can also look a bit like they have a face drawn on their backs which I always find quite amusing.

Compared to some pets such as exotic fish, these creatures are pretty easy to take care of assuming you have their set up and husbandry techniques correct from the start. They are fairly low maintenance, for instance, you don't have to spend hours taking them for walks or playing games to keep them occupied. If you go on holiday for a few days you can, in theory, set up your enclosure so that you don't need anybody to look after them which is great if your friends and family aren't as fond of arachnids as you are and saves having to pay for boarding kennels as you would a dog or a cat!

Not only do they not need constant attention but they are also fairly cheap. Whilst you can keep them in elaborate tanks it isn't necessary nor do you need to buy expensive equipment, toys, bedding and food like with some pets. In fact you can just keep them in a plastic tub with a lid as long as there are a few tiny air holes in it. A small plant (real or fake) to hide in and climb on is pretty much all the equipment they need. Attention wise you just need to provide a fresh supply of insects for food, mist their enclosures and give it the odd clean every now and then.

As mentioned previously, these spiders don't make messy webs to catch prey and whilst I'm not encouraging you to let your new pet roam around your house – this could lead to them getting injured or killed – if they did escape you probably wouldn't even notice they were there plus they'd eat all the insects that we consider pests such as flies and silverfish.

For a creature with a brain that is no bigger than a poppy seed these spiders are incredibly intelligent. Some people claim they have trained their Jumping Spiders to high five and do other tricks, whether this is true or not can't comment but I do know that scientists have trained Jumping Spiders to jump on command and have also observed them actually changing their hunting tactics according to the behavior of their prey. Their intelligence makes them fascinating to watch, especially at feeding time!

Not only are they intelligent but they each have their own personalities too and no two spiders are exactly the same. Okay as pet owners we're all guilty of attributing personalities to our pets because we desperately want them to love us as much as we love them so you might think I'm crazy if I said that whenever I hold my Phiddipus Audax on my finger he looks up at me with a pleading "love me" look with his huge watery looking eyes and maybe this is going a bit too far *but* I – and many other owners – do believe that these creatures are friendly and alert and have different personality traits, for example, some are timid and shy (not surprising given the difference between our size and theirs) whilst others are more confident and will happily march onto their owner's hands and give a little wave of their legs. There are even studies about Jumping Spiders and their varying personalities so who are we to argue with science?

Have I convinced you to buy a Jumping Spider? I hope so but it wouldn't be very responsible of me to only give the positives so now for the downsides of having this type of pet...

Firstly if you are looking for a pet that you can cuddle up with then this isn't it. Many people will say that their Jumping Spiders are friendly and love sitting on their hand and I'm not disputing this but I am inclined to believe that, like Chameleons, Jumping Spiders only really tolerate human companionship and too much contact can make them agitated and stressed out which can, in turn, lead to a shorter lifespan. A lot of owners say that their spiders appear to hate the feel of their skin and will move backwards whenever they touch them. Yes, a lot of them can be friendly and I'm not saying you should never handle them but just not every day. These spiders are incredibly fast and not that easy to handle and although some will just sit on your hand and look up at you others will run off and due to their small size they are likely to be lost or hurt if handled constantly. I would also be wary of letting children handle them for this reason as well.

For a pet, Jumping Spiders have such short lifespans that you may wonder what the point is? Hopefully I will have answered this already when I listed the reasons why they made good pets but it can be incredibly frustrating and sad when you spend time and money designing a wonderful habitat for them, set up food colonies and become attached only for your new friend to die a few months later. Whilst they don't have to cost a lot of money the bond and time factors can often be higher than the monetary cost but you should be prepared for the worst to happen just in case.

Another downside is that these spiders love live prey in the form of flies, crickets, mealworms, moths, maggots and so on so if you're a bit squeamish then this pet isn't for you. It can be a bit yucky, especially as the cheapest way of feeding is to either catch insects yourself from outside or breed your own insect colonies. Some owners say you can give your Jumping Spiders dead bugs but they won't all eat them, plus they are natural hunters and will enjoy the thrill of the chase so live insects are always better to keep them active both in body and mind. If your Jumping Spider is getting on in years or is a bit unwell then you may even have to maim or kill a bug and feed it immediately either using your fingers or tweezers. I've known people to pull legs off crickets, wings from moths or squish blue bottle flies or waxworms to feed their Jumping Spiders who weren't up to hunting. Again if you don't want to do this then I wouldn't recommend this type of pet.

It is not uncommon for these spiders to lay hundreds of eggs which can in turn end up with hundreds of babies. Now you may not be intending to breed your spider and if you purchase from a reputable breeder this shouldn't be an issue however it is worth thinking about if you are going to catch a wild Jumping Spider. These babies can also escape their enclosures fairly easily. You may be happy having one spider in your house but would you be happy with hundreds of the little creatures roaming around?

Personally I think the positives outweigh the negatives when it comes to Jumping Spiders and if you are looking for a pet that is unusual then they can become a talking point in your house. If you prefer a pet that is interesting to watch rather than one that you can handle all the time then these are fantastic.

One Spider Or Two?

You can have as many Jumping Spiders as you wish but just don't keep them in the same enclosure… remember that in the wild if they want to get away from another Jumping Spider they have acres of space in which to do so; in a small enclosure it is an entirely different story and whether you keep two females, two males or a male and female together it will all end in a similar situation with one spider being killed and possibly eaten by the other.

You could make a nice room feature by stacking several spider condominiums together and having a different Jumping Spider in each.

Of course to breed you will need to put a male and female together but you would do so only for a short period of time. Even in this scenario it can have very differing results and many breeders have lost many male spiders during the breeding process! (For more information refer to Chapter Eleven: Breeding).

Do Jumping Spiders Bite?

Yes, Jumping Spiders have small fangs which they use to bite their prey thus injecting venom and killing whatever hapless insect happened to catch their eye.

The good news is that their venom is not harmful to humans and so they are perfectly safe to keep as pets and to handle with bare hands.

Now that doesn't mean that these spiders would never bite a human, just that it shouldn't kill you or make you ill unless you are allergic to their venom. Their fangs can draw blood, similar to if you had been pricked with a pin and has been described as a sharp stab followed by a needle like pain radiating through the limb that has been bitten – for example, if you get bitten on the finger which is the most likely scenario then the pain would radiate up your arm for a few minutes. The pain does fade fairly quickly although the area that received the bite may feel sore even several hours later and although it isn't harmful it can be more painful than you would imagine a bite from such a tiny creature could be.

Jumping Spiders do have a threat posture so if you see your new pet with their front end slightly elevated with the chelicerae fully exposed showing their mouth parts then I would leave well alone. This threat posture is very unusual however, especially in the presence of humans and most of Jumping Spiders will often just retreat and run rather than start a fight but, as mentioned previously, they all have their own personalities so if you do happen to have a particularly aggressive one, this may be something to watch out for. Often females will adopt this threat pose if you disturb them whilst they are guarding eggs.

A Jumping Spider will only bite as a last resort when feeling very threatened so always handle with care. They do use their fangs for support so you may get an accidental nip if they are on your hand and feel like they are going to fall off so again be very careful when handling them. I would always advise that you handle them in an area where you can sit with your hand over a surface such as a table, container, carpet or flooring or even your knee so that they don't have far to fall if they do lose their footing.

One more thing to be aware of is that although the venom from a Jumping Spider isn't harmful to most humans some of us can be hypersensitive to spider venom. You may develop this hyper sensitivity after a single dose too so if you do happen to get bitten once this could stimulate an autoimmune response causing limbs to swell or other symptoms. Many people believe that Salticids don't produce enough venom to directly destroy very much of our tissue but our bodies autoimmune response could still be destructive so if you do get a bite that seems unusually painful or you suffer from swelling then it is worth a trip to your doctor just to be on the safe side.

Cost

This is a difficult one with regards to Jumping Spiders because in effect you could find a spider outside, put it in a plastic container you have lying about and catch insects yourself to feed it which in essence means your new pet would be free!

Of course, not everyone is living in an area where Jumping Spiders run wild or maybe you want one that isn't native to your country of origin and you may want to buy an enclosure to make it a feature in your lounge or another room in your house.

The following are costs associated with purchasing a Jumping Spider, assuming that you are buying everything new. (Please note that all prices are correct at the time of writing)

Firstly there's the spider itself. In the UK, depending on the type you want, a Jumping Spider will cost around £15 - £20 each.

Some breeders will do a deal such as £15 for one, £25 for two and £50 for three. This is cost effective but if it is your first jumper I would recommend you probably only buy one just to make sure you can successfully look after it. The last thing you want is to purchase three only for them all to die because you haven't perfected your husbandry techniques.

Also be aware that some will charge around £8.50 for delivery although if you collect at a reptile show you can avoid this but will need to pay ten percent of the price upfront as a deposit.

In the USA a Jumping Spider will cost around $14.99 or more depending on the type you want; again this is from a reputable breeder and the juveniles they are selling are from a well-known family line of Jumping Spiders with proven stock.

Now you may have read the above and be thinking 'this is wrong because I've seen Jumping Spiders in the USA for $8 or less'. I'm not doubting this is true – I have also seen these advertisements however many of them state that the spiders are 'field caught' which means you have no way of knowing their age or where they have been caught from.

The next cost to consider is the enclosure. As mentioned previously you could make an enclosure for a few pounds/dollar if you used a plastic deli cup and things you find around the house but this section is just going to assume that everything is store bought so the prices are relating to enclosures that have been made specifically with Jumping Spiders in mind.

In the UK a Jumping Spider enclosure will cost around £15.99 upwards. In the USA they can cost around $17.99 - $25.99 upwards depending on whether you want to have them custom made so that you choose your own size and colours.

You will also need to decorate your enclosure. As there are a vast amount of things you can use in your Jumping Spider's new home I cannot possibly list everything so this cost is just an estimate. As long as you have something for your spider to climb on, a flower or something for it to hide in and something that will provide shade then you can pay as much or as little as you like. Again you can buy new or scavenge from around the house; items that you can use include artificial flowers, live plants, cardboard tubes and so on. (See Chapter

4: Enclosures) My guess is that if you were to buy all your decorations new you can probably decorate a Jumping Spider's enclosure for around £5 or $5 upwards depending on how elaborate you want it to be.

A must-have is a misting bottle with a nozzle that only gives a fine spray. These can be bought in the UK for around £1.86 and in the USA for around $2.49. A word of caution; you can buy cheaper spray bottles but make sure they are a super fine mist rather than just normal misting otherwise the droplets might be too big for your teeny tiny Jumping Spider.

The final cost I can think of that is associated with a Jumping Spider is food. These creatures eat live prey so food could either be a one off cost if you buy and then use this to make your own culture; fruit flies and flies are fairly easy to breed and you can have a constant supply if you wished to do so but if don't like the thought of live bugs in your house then these would be a recurring cost meaning you would have to keep purchasing food every time you run out.

In the UK housefly maggots can cost anywhere between £2.95 - £7.98, blue bottle spikes can cost between £2 - £8 and wax worms can cost between £2.30 - £10 and crickets cost around £1.74 depending on the volume.

A live fruit fly culture will cost around £2.50 - £4.50 depending on how large a tub you use.

In the USA Bluebottle spikes will cost anywhere between $14.99 - $27.99, Waxworms cost $15.99 – 44.99, flightless fruit flies cost around $21.39 and crickets cost around $7.99, again depending on the amount that you purchase.

I estimate that to feed your feeder insects will cost around £2/$2.60.

It is worth noting that it is difficult to compare the UK and the USA prices as the UK sell by volume whereas the USA sell by amount, for example in the UK you would have the choice of 30mls or a pint of blue bottle spikes whereas in the USA you can choose between 250, 500, 1000, etc.

Just keep in mind that if you breed your spiders then these costs will increase enormously unless you start your own fruit fly culture because baby Jumping Spiders eat a lot!

On the whole, as far as pets go these are fairly cheap as you don't really have vets bills – sadly once something is seriously wrong with your spider it is usually too late to do anything about it – and you don't have associated costs such as blankets, toys, treats and so on.

As mentioned before if you use things around the house and set up your own insect cultures then you can keep costs incredibly low.

Arachnophobia

There is no denying that if you see some photographs of Jumping Spiders close up they are super cute and it is clear why some people refer to them as 'spider puppies' or 'octo-kittens' because they really do look more like a fluffy pet than a scary spider. For this reason many people who would class themselves as having Arachnophobia – a fear of spiders – actually consider buying these to keep as pets.

Whilst I believe that they can help people to conquer their fear of spiders which is great – I'm all for encouraging people to take care of these creatures rather than squash them in terror – I do think that anyone who does have Arachnophobia should consider all aspects of care before they buy them. At the end of the day the safety of the spider is paramount as is the owner's piece of mind; if you have Arachnophobia could you genuinely feed them without freaking out? Would you be able to put your hand into their webbed up enclosures to clean them out? If they jumped or touched your hand would you freak out and shake them off? If you end up panicking you may end up accidentally hurting them by shaking them off your hand. These creatures are incredibly fast and can jump when you least expect it.

My advice would be that if you do want to get over your fear of spiders and you know somebody who keeps these creatures as pets then maybe ask if they will let you look at them out of their enclosure and possibly allow you to handle them if you feel ready. This would allow you to see what they are like before you had the responsibility of looking after one yourself. If you don't know anybody who keeps Jumping Spiders then maybe visit an expo or a breeder if there is one in your area and see if they would let you look at and possibly touch their Jumping Spiders to see how you react.

Many people who are scared do end up falling in love with these creatures and there are many stories online of those who have been absolutely petrified of spiders that have overcome their fear because of these beautiful Jumping Spiders. If anything is going to help you overcome your fear of spiders I believe these are the answer!

Male Or Female?

It is often very difficult to sex a Jumping Spider until they are an adult, even for those who would consider themselves experienced breeders and often breeders or those selling these creatures will put a disclosure somewhere on their website or social media page stating that they cannot guarantee the sex of the spider you receive.

Many people refer to these animals as being 'gender fluid' but really I believe it is just that due to their small size it isn't always possible to see their reproductive parts until they are much older. I have heard many stories of people saying their male spider has suddenly changed sex and vice versa and some people get very upset over the fact that they had a pet which they thought was a boy for a few months only to realize that she's actually a girl! My advice would be not to attach yourself to a Jumping Spider because of its gender but just to see them all as spiders.

As a general guide, by the juvenile stage a male will usually have bigger and longer front arms. By the time it is a sub adult its pedipalps should look like they have bulbous or 'swollen looking' ends and once mature these take on a 'scoop' like appearance. To give you an idea of shape, many people refer to these as their 'boxing gloves'

Females by comparison tend to have a stout or fuller build and typically they are larger than their male counterparts. Their pedipalps tend to be slimmer than males. Once they are fully mature the epigynum – a hardened genital opening - will be apparent on the underside of their abdomen. Once you know what you are looking for and your female is mature enough, then you should be able to see this with the naked eye.

However, unless you have two spiders of different gender to be able to compare them, you may not really be able to identify which sex you have unless you spend a long time looking at photographs of the different genders on the Internet and even then it is not always clear.

Some of the Jumping Spider species and genus have a certain look or colouration at different stages and this can be used to identify age.

Which Should I Choose?
When it comes to choosing a Jumping Spider I think whether you choose a male or female is really just personal preference.

Care wise, it doesn't make much difference as to whether you have a male or female Jumping Spider; their enclosures will be the same size, set up will be the same with regards to places for nesting, food choices, temperature and humidity are all pretty much the same so unless you have a brilliant name that would only suit a female it doesn't really make a difference.

There do appear to be some differences between the sexes, for example, males tend to have shorter life spans than females, which may be surprising to some as many people believe that the stress of egg laying would reduce the female's life but this doesn't appear to be the case with these creatures. One theory as to why males have shorter life spans is because females are far calmer whereas males are more curious and active but there are no scientific studies that I know of that prove this to be the case.

Many keepers report that their females are friendlier and less likely to run and hide and they may just prefer to sit on a hand rather than run about and explore whereas males appear to be more curious and active.

Size wise the females of the species are larger than males.

Females can be more aggressive but often this is just when they are laying and/or guarding eggs whether they are fertile or not. This can be the drawback of females because they will spend a lot of their time sitting in an egg sac, which makes it impossible for you to interact with them. Even if they haven't been mated they will still lay and guard unfertilized eggs. They tend to be more reclusive than males and this could be because male Jumping Spiders are always on the lookout for a mate and therefore are out and about more.

Females can be prettier, for example, the female regal spider has a beautiful orange body and ruby chelicerae and this can be more attractive to some yet many male species are just as cute and attractive. Again I think this is just personal preference as I love all Jumping Spiders regardless of the sex and colour.

Many people will buy one spider then decide that actually they want another so you could always buy a male then once you are confident that you can look after them properly and you have your husbandry techniques perfected, set up another enclosure and have a female then you could compare the two for yourself.

Chapter 3: Finding Your Spider

Unlike most other pets which have to be bought from a pet shop or a breeder you DON'T always have to go out and purchase a Jumping Spider; if you are lucky enough to live in a country where these arachnids are commonly found such as the USA, Australia or The Philippines, to name but a few, then you may be able to just hunt in your own back garden for one and if you are super lucky you may even find that when the weather turns cold they come into your house on their own accord, searching for shelter or warmth.

Unfortunately, if you are in the UK you won't have any choice but to buy a spider from a breeder either online or at an expo because they aren't native creatures.

Wild Caught V Captive Bred

Often you will hear environmentalists saying don't ever take wild creatures into your home yet it is fine to capture a Jumping Spider from the wild as unlike some animals that don't breed often or are at risk of becoming endangered, taking a Jumping Spider doesn't really have that much of an ecological impact. They can lay such a large amount of eggs at one time that there is not much chance of them becoming extinct.

The advantage of capturing a wild Jumping Spider is that it is free, they are fairly easy to capture and they can be found in pretty much any environment, even cities.

Of course, there are downsides to everything and this is no exception. One of the main drawbacks is that if you catch a female Jumping Spider she may already be gravid which could lead to you end up with hundreds of tiny little spiderlings to take care of. This isn't the end of the world as you could release them back out into the wild if the weather was warm enough for them but be aware that these babies are tiny and quite a few may escape their cage either through air holes that are too big or whilst you are trying to transfer them into separate containers or outside, which may result in you having quite a few Jumping Spiders roaming around your home for a while.

A responsible breeder will separate the spiderlings a short while after hatching, which means the chances of them being gravid is very slim so if you don't want to run the risk of having a pregnant spider then purchasing from a breeder may be preferable to you.

Another drawback of capturing a wild spider is you can't really determine their age so they may already be nearing the end of their life cycle. This can be upsetting if you form an attachment and find a few weeks down the line that your new pet has died because you won't really know whether they died from old age or because something wasn't quite right with your set up.

If you buy from a breeder however, then you will know exactly how old your Jumping Spider is and the breeder should even be able to tell you the exact time and date they hatched as well as how many (if any) molts they have had. This means if your spider dies you can check whether it was due to your set up and make adjustments if necessary should you purchase another Jumping Spider.

You may find that a wild caught spider isn't as 'friendly' as a captive bred one because they aren't used to human interaction. Your wild caught spider may be constantly trying to escape or can be timid or even downright unfriendly towards you which can be disheartening if you want to interact and handle them.

Those that are captive bred are often far more docile and thus easier to handle because they have been used to humans their whole life.

If you find a wild Jumping Spider then you will be limited to whatever species you can find in your garden or local area whereas if you buy from a breeder then you may have more choice over the type you want.

One word of warning however; if you do decide to catch a Jumping Spider from outside there is a risk of parasites or mites being brought in with them which can also infect any other Jumping Spiders or invertebrates that you may have; these can be deadly if not treated.

Your Jumping Spider will be kept in it's own enclosure but it is always a good idea to keep it's enclosure away from any others for a short while, even if you bought it from a breeder, just to make sure that it doesn't have any ailments that could be transferred to the others.

Even if you purchase from a breeder there is still the risk of parasites if they are selling wild caught spiders so make sure that the Jumping Spider you are purchasing is captive bred and hasn't been around any wild caught spiders.

How To Catch A Jumping Spider

This chapter assumes that you live in a country where Jumping Spiders live in the wild so if you are in England or somewhere else where Jumping Spiders aren't native then this won't be applicable to you and your only option will be to purchase your new pet from a responsible breeder.

If you are able to have a wild caught spider then the best place to search for a Jumping Spider is your own back yard or a nearby park.

These creatures are so tiny that they may be hard to spot; remember they like to climb in order to get a bird's eye view of everything so look on walls and at the top of tall grasses or flowers or in low tree branches.

Once you spot one you will need to catch it safely so make sure you are prepared.

Identify

Firstly, make sure that the creature you have found is indeed a Jumping Spider. This means that before you even go out to hunt for one you should make sure you know what they actually look like because you want to take care that you aren't disturbing other creatures that could actually be dangerous such as the Brown Recluse, Hobo Spider or Black Widow.

Remember, a Jumping Spider will have two legs at the front which are longer and will be covered in body hair to help it grip. Jumping

Spiders also have a different eye pattern to other spiders; they have eight eyes in total that go around their 'forehead' with the two front ones being larger than the rest.

If you live in a country where there are Ant Mimic Spiders or Wasp Mimic Spiders then again you want to make sure it is a jumping spider you are catching and not an actual wasp or ant that could sting or bite you.

Wear Protective Gear
Jumping Spiders aren't poisonous to humans and one biting you won't be harmful unless you are allergic but I advise that when you're outdoors looking for one you do wear protective gear because there are plenty of other insects and species of spiders out there that are poisonous and harmful to humans. You could end up with a bite or sting that, at best is very painful but at worst could be life threatening.

By protective gear I would recommend wearing long sleeved clothing, gloves and long trousers so that all your skin is covered to reduce the risk of stings and bites.

Essential Equipment
Catching a Jumping Spider in the wild isn't something you should do on a whim. Make sure you go out there with the right equipment as not only will this help you to find them easily but will also mean your spider is cared for from the moment you have caught it.

Essential equipment includes;

A magnifying glass for you to view the spiders, enabling you to both find and identify them easier; remember these spiders can be tiny!

A container with small air holes so that you can temporarily house your new pet.

Piece of paper or thin card to help you catch your spider

A torch to help you see under bushes.

A stick to help you coax the spiders out.

Sunglasses, sun hat and sun cream as well as water for you to drink if you are outside in the sun for a long time.

Catching A Jumping Spider
Once you have found a Jumping Spider you will need to get it safely into your container without causing it injury. The easiest way to do this is if the spider is on a wall. In this scenario simply place your container over the top of the spider then slowly slide your piece of paper or thin card between the wall and the spider. The spider should jump – or be gently nudged by the paper or card – into the container. Quickly flip the container over and put the lid on before your spider can escape.

Remember to put air holes in your container BEFORE you capture your spider and don't make these too big otherwise your new pet will easily escape before you get them home.

Of course you may not find a Jumping Spider just sitting on a wall waiting for you. If you are struggling to find one take your stick and start to gently tap any bushes that are around you. Look carefully and you may see one jump.

If you find a Jumping Spider this way then gently guide it into your container either using the stick or your hand.

You could even position your fingers so that they climb on; if they do then you can just drop them into your container but don't force them, remember these spiders can be timid and you don't want to hurt them.

Best Places To Look
Jumping Spiders like being up high and enjoy the sun but also like hiding places too. Suggestions for the best places to look include (but are not limited to) the following:

- Walls or other areas that are warmed by the sun – this could include the side of buildings, fences, broad leaved plants and so on.

- Look for trees with rough bark or try peeling back bark from dead trees. If you have a woodpile in your garden this can often be a magnet for Jumping Spiders.

- The underside of picnic benches.

- Amongst leaves, on low growing bushes or in grass.

Purchasing A Spider

There aren't that many options when purchasing a Jumping Spider, especially if you want a certain type. Really the only option is either the Internet or at a spider expo where you can meet breeders in person. The downside to the latter is that you may not have one nearby and/or you may have to wait a long time before any are held.

The best time to look is spring time because most Jumping Spiders have breeding cycles that are dependent on the seasons and although in captivity this can vary, a responsible breeder won't sell in the winter months because it becomes more challenging to ship them safely, likewise they won't ship during a heatwave either as it risks the spider's chance of survival.

I would always look for breeders that offer a live arrival guarantee as well as a cautionary note stating that they will only ship when it is safe for the spider to do so as this usually shows that they are concerned about these creatures well-being.

Another thing I would look for is what they ship the spider in; a reputable breeder usually states that they are going to be in an insulated shipping box along with a 72 hour heat pad if this is deemed necessary.

Personally I think for these creatures the best way to find a reputable breeder is by joining Facebook groups and adding a post asking where people purchased their spiders from. Often you will find the same few breeders being recommended depending on whereabouts you live. Recommendations are often far better as other people's experiences – both positive and negative – will be a good indicator of whether the breeder you are considering is responsible and trustworthy.

Just remember that some people on the Internet will moan about anything in great detail whilst glossing over the good so try and pick out the positives and important things before making up your mind, for instance, if eight people talk about the same breeder and they all say their spiders arrived alive, healthy and lived a fairly long time but half gave a negative review because their spider arrived later than they were promised then this isn't necessarily a reason not to use them; some breeders will ship later than they originally stated for a variety of reasons such as if the spiders weren't ready to leave or if there was a cold spell of weather that would have made shipping hazardous and so on. Often I find the breeders that have complaints against them not delivering on time are often the most responsible ones because they are putting their spiders' health before the customers impatience.

If you are on social media sites keep an eye out as to whether any breeders comment on posts with advice; sometimes people will even ask a certain person's advice and usually this is a good sign that this person is knowledgeable and trusted.

Most breeders will state that they cannot guarantee the gender of the spider they provide and whilst they may try to sex the spider sometimes it is not apparent whether it is male or female until the very final molt so I wouldn't set my heart on having a female spider as it may be disappointing to discover that it is a male.

You can just do a quick Google search as well to find websites that sell Jumping Spiders but be wary because some people will sell wild caught spiders. I wouldn't recommend these for the reasons stated above – they could be old, gravid, and so on - and also because to make any sort of profit these people will need to capture large groups of Jumping Spiders in one go which can have bigger ecological impacts than if you were just going out into your own back garden to capture one. A lot of spiders sold at expos are wild caught, even in the UK albeit they've been caught in a different country and shipped over, but it is a big problem mainly because these spiders die without any warning after a few months, weeks or sometimes even days and it is usually because they have reached old age. This can be very upsetting for anyone who has bought one as a pet.

The last thing to look out for is anyone selling spiderlings as these may be too young to be re-homed and can often die in transit or shortly after you receive them. Spiderlings have a high mortality rate anyway so always check the age of the spider you want to purchase and make sure they are large enough to eat larger prey such as green and blue bottle flies, crickets, mealworms and so on. Again, a responsible breeder will know all this anyway and will most likely give you this information without you having to ask. Never buy a spider that has been advertised as a newborn, these creatures should have had at least two or three molts before they are shipped out to you. There are many stories out there of people who have bought spiderlings only to find that some have been dead on arrival and the others have died within a few days and usually this is because they are too young to have been separated and shipped.

Store Bought Jumping Spiders

Again I'm not aware of any pet shops in the UK that sell Jumping Spiders but in the US there are a few that do. Whilst I'm not saying that you shouldn't purchase from a pet store I would err on the side of caution purely because I hear a lot of stories of spiders bought from stores that have died a few days after purchase for no apparent reason. Now these can be delicate creatures and if your husbandry techniques are a little off then this could be the reason for these unexplained deaths but if you have other spiders that you have raised successfully in the past without any problems then it may point to an issue with the spiders that are being sold in the stores.

Whether this is the way they are kept whilst they are waiting to be bought I don't know but I would always be careful and ask lots of questions if I was buying from a pet store, such as whether the spider is wild caught or captive bred, how old it is, what it eats, is it a male or female, how long have the spiders been in the store, have they had any unexplained deaths recently and so on and so forth. If the assistants can answer all your questions in a satisfactory manner then they obviously have knowledge of these creatures. If not I would probably go elsewhere as it may point to the fact that they don't really know enough about these creatures to know if they are selling healthy ones or not.

Keep in mind that it isn't always possible to determine the sex when Jumping Spiders are young so if the shop assistant claims the spider is a juvenile and is insistent that it is a male or female but doesn't explain that it isn't always obvious until the final molt then again this could point to the fact that they don't know much about these creatures.

Most Popular Species As Pets
You may be looking for an unusual and exotic pet hence why you've decided to keep a Jumping Spider but it may be wise to choose one that is known for being able to live successfully in the home, especially if you are a novice spider owner.

These include:

Phidippus Audax – Bold or Daring Jumping Spider
These are common in North America and Canada and are a great option for beginners. Depending on where you live you may find one outside and they are pretty easy to capture.

These Jumping Spiders are medium sized and are easy for even the novice owner.

Most are black with white spots or patterns (which may be orange when younger) on their abdomens or legs but some will have different colours or patterns.

Their eyes are large and watery and their bodies and legs are hairy.

The chelicerae will be bright metallic blue or iridescent green, which is unique to them.

If you are searching for one outdoors then the best place to find them will be somewhere with lush greenery. As they don't spin webs to catch prey they like wide open areas like grasslands or fields so that they have space to hunt.

Phidippus Regius – Regal Jumping Spider

Often found in the South Eastern part of the USA or places around the Caribbean basin these are larger than the Phidippus Audax and are popular due to their colouration. They require warmer temperatures and can be rather more fragile and thus more challenging to keep as pets than the Phiddipus Audax.

They also have large eyes and hairy bodies but their iridescent chelicerae are often a striking blue-violet colour.

Males are generally black with white spots and patterns whilst the females are usually grey or slightly orange in colour.

If you're searching for one in the wild they tend to be found in open areas with a few trees, plants or walls to enable them to stalk their prey from above.

Phidippus Otiosus – Canopy Jumping Spider

Typically found in the Southeastern area of the United States and – as their name suggests – love to be as high as possible. If you are searching for one in the wild, look in high places especially amongst leaves on tall trees or at the tops of fences and walls.

Due to the areas they live in the wild these Jumping Spiders need a high humidity, although they do seem to be able to manage in some less humid climates. This should be considered if you live in an area that is more dry than humid and you should check your enclosure's humidity levels daily to ensure they are living in optimum conditions.

These spiders can range in size from 8-18mm with the females being larger than their male counterparts.

They are dark brown with white hairs along their sides. Their abdomen has an orange pattern and their chelicerae is usually green or purple.

These Jumping Spiders tend to be friendly and often jump straight onto a hand if offered when they are let out of their enclosures. Just be aware that the juveniles are often very quick although they tend to slow down as they reach their final molt.

Phidippus Johnsoni – Red-backed Jumping Spider

Platcryptus Undatus - Tan Jumping Spider
Often found in North and Central America this is one of the smaller common species. Rather more docile than some of the others it can be easily captured.

Their bodies are compressed allowing them to hide under loose bark or other small places and the prominent pattern on their abdomen can make them hard to spot on mottled surfaces so if you are searching for one check carefully along tree trunks and under loose bark.

The downside to keeping this species as a pet is that to date nobody has ever successfully bred them in captivity which means if you want one as a pet then the only option is to have a wild caught one.

Salticus Scenicus – Zebra Jumping Spider
A common Jumping Spider of the Northern Hemisphere, these Jumping Spiders can be found in a various countries. Their common name was derived from their black and white coloration, which makes it look rather zebra like.

Zebra Jumping Spiders range in size from 5-9mm with the females being on the larger size and the males at the smaller end.

If you are searching for one in the wild the best places to look are on walls, plants and fences on sunny days. They often find their way into people's houses and can be found sunning themselves on window sills or hiding in corners, especially behind curtains.

As they are a smaller species they are not as easy to see and interact with and they can also escape quite easily.

The Zebra Jumping Spider is harder to keep as a pet as they need a special diet of fruit flies and other small prey so aren't recommended for a novice Jumping Spider owner. I would only recommend buying one of these if you have already successfully owned another type of Jumping Spider for a year or more.

Hyllus Diardi – Heavy Jumping Spider
Found in Asian countries such as Myanmar, Thailand and China so unless you are local to these areas your only option would be to purchase from a breeder.

It is one of the larger Jumping Spiders and can grow as big as 10mm. They have really huge bodies, large eyes and big hairy legs.
Their larger size makes them popular as pets because they are easy to see and handle compared to some other Jumping Spiders.

Chapter 4: Enclosures

You can purchase enclosures made specifically for Jumping Spiders and I personally would recommend a novice spider keeper does this for the following reasons:

Firstly, you know the enclosure is going to be right with regards to both size and ventilation and you can rest easy that your new found friend isn't going to escape.

Secondly it can make a great centre piece; if you are planning to keep your spider in the lounge or other communal space in your home rather than a spare room where only you see them then you may want something that looks smarter than a plastic cup on a coffee table. Some enclosures are customizable so you can choose different colours to suit your décor.

Some of these enclosures are also stackable so if you choose to own more than one spider you could stack a few enclosures together and make an amazing feature piece in your home.

Whatever you use to house your Jumping Spider in, make sure it has a lid, otherwise they will just wander away.

Jumping Spiders tend to nest at the highest point of their enclosure so if you aren't using an enclosure that has been built specifically for Jumping Spiders then it is always wise to put the container upside down so the lid is at the bottom as this makes it easier for you to open the container without your spider escaping and means you don't have to keep breaking their sleeping sac every time you feed or water them.

You also need to consider the following; ventilation, size and lighting.

Ventilation
A lot of people hear the word 'ventilation' and think okay, I just need to poke a few air holes in the top so that my spider can breathe.

However ventilation is far more than that.

When I say the enclosure needs to be well ventilated I mean that air should be able to move through the whole enclosure in order to get rid of smells and reduce the risk of bacteria, mould and other horrible things growing.

To give you an idea of the importance of ventilation I will borrow an analogy that I heard someone else telling a newbie Jumping Spider keeper; imagine you spent your life living in just one room without any windows or doors. You eat here, sleep here and go to the toilet here…. I would imagine that after a while it would get a bit stuffy and smelly, don't you? Well this is exactly what your spider has; just one small enclosure where they live their whole lives.

To properly ventilate your Jumping Spider's enclosure you need to create what is known as cross-ventilation (similar to the small breeze you would get in your home if you opened two windows at opposite sides of a room).

This is where the specially made Jumping Spider enclosures have the advantage because you will often find an opening on either side of the enclosure as well as on the top.

If you are making your own enclosure then cross ventilation is easy enough to do just by putting ventilation holes in different areas of your enclosure not just on the top. Jumping Spiders live outside in the wild where ventilation is not an issue so I don't believe you can ever have too much ventilation but you should note that the number of ventilation holes will affect how hot and humid your enclosure will be so if you have too many then you may struggle to keep the humidity levels high enough.

Remember your holes shouldn't be so big that your spider can crawl through and escape and also needs to be smaller than the smallest prey you will use, otherwise you might find your spider's lunch roaming around your house.

One tip if you are worried about escapees is to cover the holes in your enclosure but be careful what you use, otherwise you will defeat the object of having ventilation holes. It needs to be a material that is breathable such as ladies tights (or panty hose) as opposed to thick, non-breathable fabrics such as denim that will prevent any air getting into your enclosure.

Also ensure that whatever you use is non-toxic as you don't want to poison your spider, therefore certain plastics and screens are not recommended.

Finally it needs to be durable as you don't want to be replacing it every couple of weeks nor do you want it to continually fall off.

Metal screens are no good because they will start to rust, as you will be misting with water on a regular basis.

One way people prevent escapees is by having their spider enclosure and putting it inside a butterfly tent.

Again, if you buy a tank that has been purpose built for Jumping Spiders you will find that the openings used for ventilation are covered in a fine mesh material so this is what you are aiming to replicate.

Size
Okay so in their natural habitat size isn't an issue and many people believe that a gigantic habitat is the best thing for a Jumping Spider. What they forget is that in the great outdoors not only is there more space but there's also more insects. If your spider's enclosure is too big they will struggle to find food, especially if you are decorating their new home with plants and other décor. If they struggle to find the prey then you may also struggle, which can be dangerous because if you are feeding crickets you will need to remove them at night to prevent them from injuring your spider.

I've also known people who think the opposite is true; that these spiders are so tiny why on earth would they need much space?

The answer to this is that Jumping Spiders are very active creatures; they love to hunt for their food and need space to do this. Hunting provides them with an activity that keeps both their bodies and minds active and thus keeps them healthy.

It's fine to keep a Jumping Spider in a small plastic cup or container like a deli cup when they are babies but once they are sub-adults they should be moved somewhere bigger.

Jumping Spiders are arboreal which means they like to nest and climb up high so your enclosure should also be taller than it is wide, another reason why I don't like keeping Jumping Spiders in small, plastic containers.

I've known people say 'I've kept my Jumping Spider in a deli cup and it lived for nine months which is a long time for these creatures' and whilst I'm not disagreeing with this I do believe that new owners should be striving to keep their new pets in optimal conditions rather than conditions that are just okay. Who's to say that in a larger container those spiders that lived for nine months couldn't live for two or three years?

My recommendations are an enclosure which is around 20cm width x 20cm depth x 30cm height (approximately 8 x 8 x 12 inches) or around half a gallon.

Anything larger than one gallon is too big for an adult Jumping Spider.

Heating And Lighting
A lot of people ask whether Jumping Spiders need a special heat and light source like a Chameleon would. Generally I would say no but it does really depend on whereabouts in the world you live and how cold your home is.

Heat and light are important as it encourages them to hunt, eat and breed but the natural sunlight is far better than any artificial source for your Jumping Spider.

I would always advise that you position your container near a window or in an area of the room that gets natural sunlight or even outside for a few hours each day. However, if your spider overheats it will dry up and die so make sure that if you do give your spider natural sunlight that you are around to watch them because if the sun moves you will be putting them at risk of being in direct sunlight.

Remember, out in the wild they would be able to go up high to bask in the sun and then retreat back into the undergrowth for shade but in an enclosure they can't escape because the whole enclosure will heat up if it's left in the sun, especially if it's made of glass.

However, if you are not home during daylight hours to watch them or are too worried about your spider overheating then you could use a small LED light instead, for instance, a 50w bulb in a desk lamp positioned near your spider's enclosure will give them enough heat and light to encourage them to come out more to eat and hunt. There are LED plant growth lights that mimic natural sunlight which, if you use real plants inside your enclosure, can help keep these healthy as well.

Don't place your lights directly on the enclosure as it would block your spider's air supply; instead use a light fixture to suspend them a few inches above the spider's home.

If you are planning to breed or have numerous spider enclosures, then UV strips running above the enclosures may be beneficial.

Whether you opt for natural sunlight or artificial, my advice is to provide plants or flowers that will give your Jumping Spider some shade; these creatures love the heat and will bask at the top of the enclosure for a while but they need to be able to retreat and cool down when they have had enough.

As for temperature, a normal room temperature that is comfortable for you seems to be fine for them.

If the temperature drops suddenly, some keepers move their enclosures closer to the radiator, others like to use a small space heater or humidifier in the corner of the room. Any of these options are fine as long as you mist more often and keep an eye on humidity levels. Soaking a cotton bud (Q tip) or some cotton wool in water and placing it in the enclosure can help with humidity in this situation.

Some genus' like Hyllus Diardi and Phidippus Regius do enjoy higher temperatures but remember that if you are misting then their housing should be fairly humid and therefore warmer than the room that their enclosure is in. Whilst you may feel it is a bit cooler one day their enclosure may still be hot enough.

Usually the temperature inside their enclosures should be around 75 – 83 degrees depending on the type of Jumping Spider you have. If this is the first time you have owned one then I would recommend you purchase some gadgets to measure both humidity and temperature to ensure you get the right levels.

Some people like to use heat pads at the bottom so the spider gets warmth but can retreat to the top of their enclosure if they wish to do so. I always think this defeats the object because most of the time your Jumping Spider will like to hang out near the top of their enclosures rather than the bottom so they shouldn't have to go down for heat. I believe it is far better to create a basking spot using a light near the top of the enclosure where they can warm themselves up and then about halfway down create some shady space so your Jumping Spider can cool off once they've had enough heat and light.
If you do use a heat pad then do so with caution and don't use with plastic enclosures because when heated up, plastic can emit toxic fumes, which can be harmful for these little creatures.

Substrate
Substrate is the substance that you place at the bottom of your tank, for instance, if you owned a hamster you might want to use shredded paper as your substrate. Unlike a hamster who will use this substrate for bedding however, your Jumping Spider doesn't really need anything.

Jumping Spiders make their nests high up, usually in the top most corner of their enclosure or possibly in a leaf or around a twig or in some little hidey hole that they've found to squeeze themselves in. As mentioned before they are arboreal so won't spend a lot of time at the bottom of the tank unless they have spotted and caught prey down there.

There are a few different things you can use as substrate for Jumping Spiders and there are pros and cons to each.

Fine Soil Or Potting Soil
This is the first thing that occurs to people when they think of using substrate in a Jumping Spider's tank after all, most species of Jumping Spiders will live in a soil based habitat out in the wild.

The pros of soil is that it does mimic most Jumping Spider's natural habitat and when used with plants and flowers can provide a great focal point, making your spider's enclosure an ornament as well as a functional home.

It also makes it easier for you to keep your enclosure humid and of course if you are using real plants as opposed to artificial ones then you will need to keep them in soil.

However, many people will say to avoid soil because although it looks natural your Jumping Spider won't really use it as they spend most of their time at the top of the tank not the bottom. Soil can be messy, especially if you are using an enclosure with a lid – as I mentioned before this lid needs to be at the bottom rather than the top so every time you open it soil will most likely leak out which can be irritating to clean up constantly.

Soil is also harder to clean. Whilst you can probably remove dead prey by hand easy enough you will have to scoop out the soil and wipe down your enclosure and add clean soil on a regular basis which again is not only time consuming but means you will need to keep temporarily housing your spider elsewhere every time you clean which can be stressful for them.

Another drawback of soil is that some of the feeder insects you place in the enclosure can hide. If you don't find them then crickets that have hidden themselves could turn on your spider when they are resting or molting. Other feeders such as mealworms could bury under the soil and turn into beetles, which again pose a threat to your spider.

If your spider is brown or a dark colour, soil can make it more difficult to find them, which means you may accidentally mist them, causing them to drown.

Soil can also grow mold, especially if you live in an area that is hot or if your tank is very humid.

If you add isopods such as Springtails to your enclosure then they will help by 'cleaning up' any leftover prey, fungi or mould that may be in your enclosure. Your spider won't eat these unless it's really hungry so you shouldn't need to constantly replace them but you will have to be careful none escape when you are opening your enclosure.

In my opinion, whilst soil looks great I wouldn't recommend it if you are aiming for low maintenance.

Kitchen Roll/Paper Towel
When thinking of substrate this is probably the last thing that would occur to you but hear me out.

Kitchen roll/paper towels are cheap and easy to clean; you simply pull one out and replace it with another one.
As most kitchen roll is white it is easy to see your spider (and it's food) so you won't have to worry about anything escaping.

If your spider does get wet either by accidental misting or by getting caught in a water droplet, kitchen roll absorbs the water easily and can help it dry out quicker, thus avoiding a nasty death.

The drawbacks are that it doesn't mimic the natural habitat and admittedly it doesn't look as nice but for a low maintenance enclosure it is recommended.

No Substrate
People say it's far easier to have nothing at all in your enclosure for a Jumping Spider and this could be true, however I believe that you will need to clean the bottom more often than if you had something covering it.

Having nothing at all makes it super easy to find leftover food and there is nothing for the feeder insects to bury in so no danger of anything hiding.

The downsides are that it doesn't mimic any natural habitat.

A plastic surface can be slippery and make it difficult for a Jumping Spider to climb, especially when they start to get older and lose their grip.

Some people simply put a potted plant in the centre of their tank but of course this depends how big your enclosure is.

Shelters And Decoration
Again, many owners will say that decorations or shelters aren't necessary for the same reason given previously; Jumping Spiders will make their own silk hammock and hang out at the top of their tank. However, I dislike seeing Jumping Spider enclosures that are just empty of anything but the spider. I believe that as a responsible owner you should at least try and give them as natural an environment as possible. Okay, this may sound like I'm contradicting myself, after all haven't I *just* said that kitchen roll is unnatural yet fine to have in the bottom of an enclosure and now I'm saying make it natural? What I mean when I say "as natural an environment as possible" I simply mean giving them places to climb, provide shade in and generally hide out in like they would have in the wild.

I believe that an empty enclosure can make your spider feel very vulnerable, whereas if it has places to hide it will feel more secure and less stressed. I also think it makes their enclosure far more interesting for them to navigate and gives them more of a challenge when hunting. This provides both physical and mental stimulation, which I believe can help these creatures live longer in captivity although there is no evidence to prove or disprove this theory.

Having twigs and plants for your spider to crawl over and stalk their prey is also far more exciting for you and it is truly amazing to watch them change direction or even come to a complete stop mid-pounce in reaction to their prey's behavior.

To decorate your spider's home you can use natural materials such as wood, tree bark, twigs, small logs, leaves, plants and even flowers. If you bring anything in from outside make sure you can be confident it hasn't been sprayed with pesticides and doesn't have mould growing or any mites, parasites or other insects that could harm your spider attached to it.

Another option is to use fake flowers and plants and many people prefer this as they don't have to worry about trimming back plants when they grow too big. The only problem that may arise with fake plants and flowers is that you need to check regularly for mold. Get ones that can be cleaned easily, otherwise you will be constantly replacing them.

You can attach fake flowers or other decorations to the enclosures using a hot glue gun. This glue doesn't appear to harm Jumping Spiders as long as you do all the hot gluing then give it a few days to dry out without the enclosure lid on before you put your spider inside. This way if there were any fumes given off by the hot glue it will have had chance to dissipate.

If you do attach anything then make sure it is all secure as you don't want them to fall whilst your spider is climbing or even worse crush them whilst they are stalking their prey or having a drink.

I've seen people use little pot mushroom or fairy houses inside their Jumping Spider enclosures, similar to the type you can buy for aquariums or as garden ornaments. These look lovely but if you purchase one then keep in mind that you should be able to get in and out easily if you need to; what happens if your Jumping Spider takes prey in there yet doesn't finish it? You will need to remove it

44

otherwise it will start to rot, therefore you need to make sure this can be done without disturbing the spider constantly, especially if they make a nest inside. One without a bottom on that you can easily lift up and down to access is probably the best option.

Other good items to include are hollowed out acorns or acorn lids, pipe cleaners to climb on – the glittery ones can look like their homes are decorated with tinsel when you take close up photographs, different sized straws cut down to size, plastic or cardboard tubing or bark to name but a few. This list isn't exhaustive and you can find other bits and pieces around the house that are probably suitable if you use a bit of imagination.

An advantage to decorating your spiders home is that it gives them other items for them to nest in which means they are less likely to block the lids or opening to their enclosure with their webs.

As well as providing them with nesting places, these items should also provide them with a bit of shade should they need it.

Also keep in mind that you want to give your spider plenty to climb on, especially if they are in a glass or plastic enclosure as sometimes spiders – especially older ones – may find the walls too slippery so plenty of other items to climb means they can still hunt and roam around successfully.

One word of warning – be careful if using wood in your enclosure. Twigs from outside should be okay but if you are using things like lollipops (popsicle) sticks or thin pieces of wood like that these can become very damp with constant misting and may never dry out because of the humidity; this could cause it to grow mould or fungus.

This mould or fungus can be white, fuzzy and 'web like' so always inspect your enclosures closely. If you do find anything growing mould then remove it from the tank immediately. You may also want to increase your ventilation and mist slightly less.

One more thing I would be cautious about is using any type of paint in a Jumping Spider's enclosure as it can release toxic fumes. It may state on the packaging that it doesn't contain any large quantities of toxins, which would make it harmful to humans but this could be relative to size; painting a lollipop stick wouldn't be harmful to you but size wise it could be the equivalent of painting your sofa.

Also remember that our internal systems are very different to that of Jumping Spiders and what is harmful to them may well have no effect on us. Let's be honest, nobody is really testing the effects of acrylic paint on Jumping Spiders to see if it's safe. Painting your enclosure or any item in it is basically a risk, are you willing to take it? I personally am not and err on the side of caution, as I don't want to risk the health of my pets. I never use anything in my Jumping Spider's enclosure that I wouldn't put inside a fish tank.

If you did decide you wanted to take the risk then look for paint that has a VOC of less than fifty. Some paints have a VOC of zero and of course these would be even better. However, it is not something I endorse either way.

There are many safer ways to achieve a colourful enclosure; for instance you could hang ribbons around, glass aquarium pebbles, colourful flowers and plants, pipe cleaners and so on.

Chapter 5: Settling In

Regardless of where your spider comes from and whether it was wild caught or bought from a breeder, chances are that it will be stressed and overwhelmed by the time it reaches your home; if you have caught your new pet yourself then you have removed it from the environment it knew well to a completely unfamiliar territory and if you have bought it from an expo or a breeder then chances are it has been transported quite a lot over large distances. Even if you have found it inside your home it could still be stressed from cold, hunger and/or thirst.

Firstly you need to re-home your spider into the larger enclosure. I would always recommend that you have this 'forever home' set up before you bring your spider home so that all you have to do is put it inside.

One important thing to note here is; DO NOT OPEN THE CONTAINER that your spider is in. You need to locate your spider first for the following reasons;

1. Your spider could jump out and escape with or without you noticing.

2. Jumping Spiders like to make their sacs at the highest point of their home. If they have made one of these sacs whilst being transported to your home it could be a molting sac and if you rip the lid off without checking, you risk interrupting a molt which can have serious health impacts and in some cases can even lead to death.

3. You will need to mist the container and if you don't locate your spider first you could end up spraying them directly, which could kill them.

Once you have located your spider you can decide what to do next.

If they are in the lid or a sac then you simply have to wait for them to leave. However, you do need to mist and one common mistake new spider owners make is that they are told to "leave their new friend alone" and take this literally only to return a few days later and find that their spider has dried out from lack of moisture.

To mist simply spray water through the ventilation holes of the container your spider is in. Make sure that you always mist the sides opposite to where your spider is. You can buy a spray bottle suitable for misting online or from any hardware store; check the nozzle before you purchase however, as the finer the mist the better as these tiny spiders can drown in large droplets.

DON'T EVER SPRAY THE SPIDER DIRECTLY.

Your spider may venture out of its nest immediately or it could take a long time, especially if they are in molt but it is important that you let them come out in their own time so be patient and go off and do any tasks you can find to keep yourself busy whilst you wait for your new friend to emerge. (Don't forget to mist daily or however often is necessary depending on the climate).

If you have located your spider and they aren't in a sac then you can transfer them to the larger container.

Chances are you are going to be super excited and want to play with your new friend immediately, but you should try and let them venture into their new home and get settled first. Remember at this point they won't know if you are a friend or a predator and they will no doubt be wary of you. Letting them get used to their new environment in their own time will help reduce their stress levels, which is better for their health.

To get them out of the small container they travelled in and into their new home, firstly mist the sides of the container you are going to put them in. If the temporary container is small enough to fit inside their new, larger home then you can simply take the lid off and place the whole container in, resting it gently on its side to make it easier for your new spider to crawl out. If the temporary container is too big to fit inside you will need to gently coax your new friend out. The best way to do this is to try and get them to climb on something like a thin paintbrush, twig or flower then transferring this into the new home.

If you want to handle your spider then you could even put your finger in and see if they will jump onto this first. Your Jumping Spider may be happy to interact with you immediately and if this is the case then great, let them climb on your finger and have a good look at you but don't handle them for too long. Carefully place them into their new home before they can run away.

Once they are in their new home give them some food, preferably something small like a fly or two, close their enclosure and walk away.

Chapter 6: Feeding

In the wild, insects comprise the majority of a Jumping Spiders diet, although some genus have been known to take nectar from wild flowers but for those that you keep at home as pets you will need to have live insect colonies ready for whenever your spider is hungry.

Crickets
These are usually the main option for Jumping Spiders in captivity because they can be found pretty much anywhere both in local pet shops or online.

Depending on whereabouts in the world you live it may be possible to catch crickets out in the wild although many keepers will advise against this as there is a higher risk of parasitic infections being passed onto your spider.

If you're not too squeamish and wish to save a bit of money, they are pretty easy to raise at home.

The downside to feeding crickets is that they can turn on your spider and bite them. Only put in one at a time and if your spider doesn't eat it then make sure that the cricket is removed before your spider rests.

If you are taking crickets from outside then make sure they are small ones, likewise if you are ordering online you will find a variety of sizes. Pinhead or small black crickets are always the best options for your Jumping Spider, otherwise they may struggle to kill them.

Crickets can kill a Jumping Spider, especially if they are old or molting so I would always recommend that you keep an eye on your Jumping Spider when feeding to make sure this doesn't happen, at least in the beginning until you know your new pet can tackle them safely.

The advantage of cultivating your own crickets is that you can feed them before they get too big for your spider thus reducing the risk of them attacking. However, many people don't like raising live crickets because of the noise they make; their chirruping can be incredibly loud!

Whilst I prefer live prey because it gives the spiders the thrill of the hunt, some Jumping Spiders will eat food that has been freshly killed so you could try and kill or maim a cricket before feeding it to your spider if you are worried. Just be careful if you do this because they are pretty tough cookies; I have seen crickets that have had their hind legs pulled off and their heads nearly dislocated still able to run around holding their heads with their front legs and attack Jumping Spiders! However, crickets without heads cannot do any harm so although this may sound gruesome if you are going to kill a cricket for your spider I would take the head off completely.

As it's thought to be the movement of the prey that attracts the Jumping Spiders you may find that your new pet has no interest in the cricket you have squashed for them; you could try and wiggle it about with your fingers or tweezers to give the impression that it is moving to encourage your spider to pounce on it.

Flies
Jumping Spiders love flies so it is a good idea to have a steady supply if possible. They are also a great food source because they are high in nutritional value.

Again, these can be found readily in pet stores and online. The best ones are house flies, blue bottles or green bottles or for smaller spiders like babies and juveniles, flightless fruit flies.

Even ones that find their way into your home are suitable to feed to your Jumping Spider if you can catch them. Outside it may prove difficult to manoeuvre the flies into a container.

As well as not being easy to catch, flies aren't that easy to raise either but a single online order can last a month or more given the proper care.

The best way to keep flies is to mix sugar or anything sweet with warm water and place in a small cup. Use a paper towel to soak up the sugary water (otherwise the flies will drown) then let the flies feed from it, after a few hours place it all, flies and all, into the fridge.

The flies should stay alive for a few weeks in the refrigerator but if they are dying too quickly then your fridge could be too cold. The front tends to be a bit warmer so either place your fly container near the front or adjust the temperature of the fridge, just be careful you don't make it too warm otherwise your food might go bad! A lot of people find that it is best to keep their flies in the vegetable drawer of the fridge – of course don't put your vegetables in there with them!

The coldness of the fridge dulls their senses and slows them down which means you can take them out, one or two at a time either by hand or with tweezers without worrying about them all escaping and buzzing around your head every time you open their container.

Some people don't like keeping flies in the refrigerator for obvious reasons but if you keep them at room temperature they can lay eggs which turn into maggots. You can feed these maggots – or spikes as they are also known - to your Jumping Spider but be aware that within a week or so they will turn into pupae and then into flies.

An advantage to flies is that they can't harm your spiders even those that are old, ill or molting.

Mealworms
Another great delicacy your Jumping Spider will love are mealworms. Again, they are easy to source both online and in local pet stores. They are also not high maintenance so you can easily set up your own food colony if you wished to do so.

Mealworms may not be interesting to some Jumping Spiders because they don't move as much as other prey do which means your new pet may just ignore them altogether.

Always remove uneaten mealworms from your spider's enclosure otherwise if you use substrate such as sand, soil or bark they can burrow and will eventually turn into beetles which are both aggressive and dangerous to Jumping Spiders.

52

Dubia Roaches

Many Jumping Spiders will accept these critters and again they are sold in many local pet stores, online and are also easy to keep should you wish to set up your own colony.

The downside is that many can burrow in substrate and hide from the Jumping Spider, later turning on them when they are more vulnerable such as when they are sleeping or molting.

Some Dubia Roaches may also be too big for your Jumping Spider so it is not always recommended that you buy them online.

Waxworms

Waxworms are the caterpillar larvae of wax moths and are high in fat and calories and pretty much low in everything else. Think of them as the spider equivalent of chocolate or chips; whilst they are great to give as a treat you shouldn't make these a staple food in your Jumping Spider's diet. Too many waxworms can lead to malnutrition. However, what many owners do is buy waxworms, feed a few to their spider and then let them pupate into moths, which are healthier for your spider.

Moths

I don't personally think these are great creatures to raise yourself but you can find them outside on an evening or even roaming around your house. You can also buy in pet shops and online.

The reason why moths are so good is that they cannot bite or attack your spider in any way.

Preferences

The insects listed above are the main ones that are recommended for Jumping Spiders although you may find more suggestions on the Internet such as locusts.

You may find that your Jumping Spider has its own preference on what it eats, for example some species like the Phidippus Ostiosus (The Canopy Jumper) may refuse crickets and other non-flying prey whereas other Jumping Spiders may kill flies because their buzzing irritates them yet not eat them at all.

It would be wise to give your Jumping Spider a variety of insects when it is old enough for them and see what they prefer before you start large colonies, for instance, if you have a Jumping Spider that doesn't like crickets there is no point in starting your own cricket colony.

I would always try to give a mixed diet if possible but it won't hinder your Jumping Spider's health if you give the same food for a few days in a row whilst you are waiting for other feeders. The only one I wouldn't do this with is wax worms.

You could even post on forums and social media sites asking what other owners who have the same type of Jumping Spider as you feed theirs.

Jumping Spiders feed by sucking the liquid out of their prey rather than eating the whole thing; if you don't have any cage cleaners in your enclosure, always remove leftover food to avoid mould. Whilst some Jumpers will return to the remains of a carcass most won't because their hunger is visually stimulated.

Many people new to keeping these pets will see their spiders getting really fat abdomens and panic that they are over feeding them. Jumping Spiders won't in fact overeat and will stop when full. If your spider is getting very large then continue to feed them as this is often just a sign that they are going to molt or if they are female they could be about to lay eggs. Once they make an egg or a molt sac they will stop eating for a few days.

What To Avoid

There are some things you should never give Jumping Spiders though and these are beetles, ants, fireflies and other spiders – whether you know what type they are or not. Not only could some of these creatures be poisonous they may also be aggressive and turn on your spider or have defense mechanisms that are harmful. For example, a tiny ant may not affect you at all but it could spray acid on your Jumping Spider.

Woodlice won't hurt your Jumping Spider and they are great to use as 'clean up' insects in your cage but I wouldn't use them as a food source because their shell is very difficult to penetrate.

Supplements
Although nobody has proven that additional supplements are harmful to Jumping Spiders they simply aren't necessary so I would avoid dusted feeders. The best way to give your Jumping Spiders the nutrients they need is to properly care for the feeder insects and feed them up well before feeding them to your pet.

Size Progression
It is important that you give your Jumping Spider the correct size prey; too big and your spider will struggle to kill it and may end up being hurt or killed. Too small and your spider will be hungry which could lead to health issues. A general rule of thumb for feeding is to never feed your Jumping Spider anything more than one and a half times their size.

You may hear a lot about 'instars' when you are searching for Jumping Spider information, for example 'first instar' 'third instar' and this is the developmental stage between molts. For instance, a first instar Jumping Spider is one that has just hatched out of the egg. A second instar is one that has had it's first molt, third instar is after it's second molt and so on.

The following is a list of suggested prey depending on the stage your Jumping Spider is at.

1st Instar – As this is a spider that has just hatched it shouldn't have ventured out of its nest yet so often it just eats the webbing that the mother made the egg sac or nest from.

2nd to 3rd Instar – flightless fruit flies like Hydei or Melongasters

3rd to 4th Instar – Hydei fruit flies, house flies.

4th to 5th Instar – house flies, blue bottles, spikes, wax worms, crickets, etc.

Once you have started to give your Jumping Spiders larger prey such as crickets, house flies or blue bottles and they have successfully hunted and killed them then you do not have to revert back to feeding them fruit flies. For older spiders these won't provide enough nutrition and will leave them hungry unless you give a huge amount. The only time that you may want to start giving fruitflies again is if your Jumping Spider is very old and has stopped eating everything including 'easy' prey like bluebottles.

You may find that when you first give your Jumping Spider bigger prey than fruit flies it may be a little wary or even appear frightened. Watch your Jumping Spider closely as they can be really fascinating; usually they will study the prey and work out how to take it down.

One phenomenon that has occurred in recent years is that some Jumping Spiders won't ever eat live prey and this appears to be based on how domesticated they are. A wild spider most likely will always prefer live over dead unless it is very old and is struggling to hunt but some breeders who are doing studies on these creatures have noticed that their third generation spiders appear to find it more difficult to hunt and kill prey than their ancestors did and may continually run away and hide from live prey. If this happens, you will need to pre-kill the prey and just wiggle it around either using your fingers or tweezers to get your spider's attention. It is always wise to watch your spider when feeding to see how it reacts to prey and to make sure it doesn't end up being food itself.

Another theory for Jumping Spiders not hunting is because they become used to 'human interference'; they run away from something they are a bit scared of, you catch this prey and kill it, they jump down and eat it from your hand. If this is true then it is just another demonstration of how clever these creatures really are that they recognize when someone is helping them.

Whatever it is, as the spider gets older they may become more adept at hunting but if they don't then you will just have to give them a helping hand and is a great way to interact and form a bond with them.

When To Feed
Jumping Spiders don't need to be fed every day. It is recommended that you offer food every three days but even then don't worry if they don't eat every time you feed them; some just have bigger appetites than others.

How often they will eat depends on a variety of things such as the sex, age and species of the Jumping Spider, for example, a female will usually eat more than males because they produce eggs regardless of whether they are fertilized or not.

Young spiders tend to eat more than old ones because they are growing. Indeed third and fourth instars can eat from three to four fruit flies per day so I would recommend that at this age you put in three or four fruit flies per spider in once a day. Some may die before they are eaten but this is better than not feeding enough.

Spiders who are sitting on eggs or who are molting may go weeks without eating and older adults can go for as long as a month without food.

Unless it has been more than three weeks I wouldn't generally worry about your spider, chances are it's just not hungry but if you do want to encourage them to eat then you could try feeding different prey just in case they don't like the food you have put in with them.

If you are feeding live prey (which is recommended) then the best time to put it in would be in the morning as this gives your spider all day to hunt and eat which is the time when they are most active.

At night, remove any uneaten prey as this can disturb your spider at night and may even attack them whilst they are resting.

How To Feed
Simply drop the feeder insect into your enclosure and wait. If you can be around when you feed your spider rather than just dropping in

food and leaving then it is well worth it because their hunting techniques truly are fascinating.

Once your Jumping Spider has finished eating then remove whatever is left because otherwise it will start to rot and make the cage smelly.

You can teach your Jumping Spider to take food directly from your hand if you aren't squeamish about touching live prey. If you don't want to do this you could use tweezers to hold the food for your spider.

There is nothing wrong with feeding your Jumping Spider by hand, indeed it can be fun BUT don't do it for every meal as hunting keeps your Jumping Spider active both in body and mind and they need to hunt for themselves in order to stay healthy.

Feeders

There is no way around it; if you are keeping Jumping Spiders you will need to feed and keep the insects they eat as well.

The ideal way to feed your Jumping Spiders would be to raise colonies of different insects as it works out cheaper in the long run and you always have a steady food supply.

Even if you don't want to raise colonies of insects and prefer to purchase insects as needed either online or in a local pet shop, you will still need to keep and feed these insects until your spider is ready to eat them because Jumping Spiders are hunters and need live prey.

This means you need to house your feeder insects correctly and whilst a lot of people do keep them successfully in plastic tubs I would always recommend purchasing some sort of housing that is designed for keeping feeder insects as this way you can be certain they will last longer.

You also need to feed these insects correctly as this is the best way to give your new pet the nutrition it needs.

Just one word of warning; if you plan to catch your feeder insects in the wild rather than raise them yourselves then you need to consider what you will do when the weather turns colder as you may not be able to find the correct insects outside as easily.

Flightless Fruit flies
Many people are surprised to find that flightless fruit flies actually have wings; thankfully these appendages don't function in a way that allows them to fly but this doesn't mean they can't escape, in fact the opposite is true and if you are not careful you could find yourself over run.

Usually if you buy in a pet store or online fruit flies will come in a jar. The problem arises when you want to get three or four out of the jar to feed to your Jumping Spider without the rest escaping. Many keepers hear the word 'flightless' and unwittingly unscrew the lid expecting the tiny little creatures to be sat at the bottom. What they don't expect is for them to be active and at the top of the jar ready to hop out when the lid is removed!

If you don't want a face (or house) full of fruit flies then luckily there are several ways to avoid this.

Firstly, slap the top of the lid before you remove it to knock any flies that are in the lid down to the bottom then start lightly tapping the jar on a surface; this knocks all the fruit flies that are climbing up the side down as well. If you are feeling brave you can continue lightly tapping the jar then quickly tip the jar over the enclosure and put the lid back on.

If you are feeling really brave you could just tap the container rather than the lid and just remove and quickly shake the lid itself into the spider's enclosure – usually doing this you get around twenty fruit flies, which is great if you have four or five small Jumping Spiders that have been housed together because they have only recently hatched but for someone that only owns one spider,mthis could be too much however and more fruitflies may end up dying from lack of food before your Jumping Spider gets round to eating them. This is not only is a waste but also means you have more cleaning up to do as you will need to remove them before they start to rot.

If you are using the tapping method, then you need to be really quick because it only disorientates them for a few seconds; once the tapping stops they will surge to the top again.

Coldness slows them down so it is wise to put them in the fridge for around 5 – 15 minutes to dull their senses then you can tap a few onto a piece of paper or into a separate container. If you use a separate container then coat the sides a few inches from the top with Vaseline or olive oil as this will prevent them from climbing out of the tub as they will be unable to get passed this line. However, whilst it will provide you with a bit of extra time don't put too many in just in case one or two are particularly determined to get out regardless.

One clever trick I have seen on social media which seems to work well is to freeze a container and put ice inside it, take the flies out of the fridge and pour in the amount you need inside this iced container. This then keeps them cool for a longer period of time allowing you to get them to your spider's enclosure without them suddenly heating up and making a quick getaway.

Another way of getting fruit flies out of the jar is to use the tapping or fridge method but instead of pouring them out, use an aspirator or pipette to suck them up. You can even make your own by covering one end of a straw with a paper towel or piece of nylon then putting this end in your mouth, putting the open end into the fly jar and sucking. Once over the spider enclosure simply stop sucking and if needed gently blow or squeeze the fruit flies out. Just make sure that you secure the end with the nylon or paper towel on with a rubber band or something similar otherwise you could find yourself snacking on a mouthful of fruit flies.

Whatever method you use I would always recommend to carry it out over the sink; this way if you do lose some you can simply wash them down the drain; yes it's a bit of a waste but it's better than ending up with a swarm of fruit flies living in your home.

Going On Holiday

If you want a few days away then you would usually put your pet in some sort of pet shelter like boarding kennels or maybe even with a friend or family member. With a Jumping Spider there are no boarding facilities and some of your friends and family may be too squeamish to want to offer to look after your new pet, especially if they have an aversion to the feeder insects too.

However, don't despair because these creatures can usually be left alone for a few days without any harm coming to them because they don't need feeding every day and will be quite happy just roaming their enclosure; most likely won't even notice you're gone.

If you are just going away for a night then you can feed your Jumping Spider before you leave, mist and leave a wet paper towel or cotton ball or similar in their enclosure for water and humidity.

Should you be going for longer then you may need to take a little bit more care over your set up but it is do-able.

Food wise it is fairly easy to leave these creatures for a week, assuming they are not early instar and are able to eat bigger prey such as blue bottles. Simply leave a few blue bottle pupae and spikes in the spider's enclosure. Your Jumping Spider will be able to eat the pupae and spikes as they are but these will also hatch at differing times so the pupae will usually hatch first turning into spikes, which in turn will morph into bluebottles.

Try to calculate as best you can how many you will need otherwise if you put too many in they may all hatch and annoy your Jumping Spider by buzzing around, especially if you don't have a large enclosure. Also, if they manage to escape then you could end up with a lot of flies roaming your house.

Usually for a pet you would imagine that more food would be better than less food but in this case less is definitely better because these creatures can go a week without food.

I would look at how many flies your spider eats in a week, remember they often only eat every two to three days so if your spider ate two every other day and you were going away for seven days then this would be fourteen in a week. Therefore, if you fed your spider either the same day or the day before you leave then you would probably only want to put in around ten pupae/spikes in total.

The complicated part is actually water because of course you should be misting your enclosure every day or every other day depending on the humidity of the area you live. Of course your spider won't suddenly miraculously be able to go a week without misting just because you are away so how do you get around this?

One way is to set up a dripper system, which slowly drips water into the tank. I have seen this done with a paper or plastic cup with a tiny hole poked into the bottom and suspended above the spider's enclosure. Assuming you have ventilation holes in the top of your enclosure, which you should have, then the water should slowly drip down through these holes and into your spider's enclosure.

If you were to make your own dripper system I would be very careful about checking it before you leave to make sure it works as if you poke too big a hole then your Jumping Spider may end up being drowned if it is dripping too quickly or the drops of water are too large.

Another option is to buy a mister system which mists regularly, these are used for reptiles so I would always make sure it is suitable for the size of your enclosure and again check that it is a fine mist.

Once you have a dripper or misting system set up this will provide drinking water as well as your spider will drink the droplets. Mist before you leave and put some wet paper towels folded up in a corner of the tank or cotton wool balls or cotton swabs (Q tips) just to help with humidity and for your spider to drink from if it wishes too.

Finally, leave a desk lamp or lights either suspended above your enclosure or near to it and put these on a light timer so that your spider has heat and light to help it hunt. This is better than leaving the enclosure by the window as you won't be around to move it should it get to hot or if the sun moves the enclosure is then at risk of direct sunlight exposure.

Again, make sure that your set up is safe and the light isn't too hot or bright for the size of your enclosure before you leave.

I would suggest you set everything up at least a couple of weeks before you are due to leave and then start the dripper system and lighting timer a week before you go so that you are still around should anything go wrong. If it isn't correct then you are able to change things before anything detrimental happens to your spider.

Chapter 7: Water

Jumping Spiders breathe through 'book lungs', which are located in their abdomens. These structures got their name as they look similar to the pages of a book; if a spider's abdomen gets wet the water can get between the 'pages' and thus suffocate them, which is why you should never spray a spider directly.

Misting

Misting means spraying your spider's enclosure with a spray bottle that has a very fine nozzle; the reason I say very fine nozzle and I really can't stress this enough is because your spider could drown even in a droplet. What doesn't look big to you can in fact be huge to your spider so even if you have a spray bottle at home that you think you can use please make sure it only sprays out a very fine mist. One's used to spray hair, for example, are not recommended.

Also, if you are using one that you have at home make sure it hasn't had any type of disinfectant or chemicals inside it, for example, recycling a cleaning product spray bottle or one used to kill weeds when gardening isn't recommended as even when empty there could be a residue inside the bottle that could harm your spider.

There are two important reasons for misting; firstly it gives your spider something to drink, secondly it increases humidity levels to prevent your spider from drying out.

To mist, simply spray one side of your enclosure, away from the spider and it's nest. If you have live plants then spray the bottom as well as the leaves.

Humidity

There is very conflicting advice when it comes to misting for humidity and this can make it very confusing; should you mist daily or even twice a day or just three or four times a week?

The reason why there is no one definitive answer is because it's like asking someone 'how long is a piece of string?' The answer will be different for everyone because it depends on your location and how humid the natural environment is as well as how much ventilation your enclosure has.

For example, in the UK it isn't humid at all, say I lived here and you said to me 'how many times a day do you mist?' I might say, at least twice a day yet you might live in Florida or somewhere that is naturally humid most days and therefore find that this is far too much.

Likewise, we could both live in the UK and yet your enclosure could be a deli cup or a specially made spider enclosure that holds humidity well and my spiders could be housed in butterfly nets, again this means that I would be misting far more often than you because the butterfly net won't hold humidity as well.

For those living in the UK, remember that your spider doesn't originate from here and its natural environment often is hot, humid places like Florida or bordering states or Cuba or the Bahamas, et cetera all with more tropical environments and this is what you are aiming to recreate.

The best advice I can give you with regards to misting is to buy a gadget that monitors humidity and check that the humidity levels are around 50-60%. If your spider is molting I would probably up these humidity levels slightly just to make sure that their molt doesn't get stuck.

Just remember, too dry an environment will dehydrate your spider whereas too wet an environment will encourage mold and could cause your spider to drown. You are aiming for a dry moist cycle – spray the enclosure then let it dry out before you spray again. Keep an eye on how long it take for your enclosure to dry out, if it took two hours, say then you need to mist every two hours, if it took a day and a half then you only need to spray once a day or once every other day.

Soil and live plants help to keep humidity but if you don't want to have worry about the upkeep of live plants then place a wet paper towel or wet cotton balls inside as this will help hold the humidity.

How Do I Give My Spider A Drink?

Your spider will drink the droplets from misting; any water that's on plant leaves or at the side of the tank will be good for your spider to drink.

Another way of giving your spider a drink is to soak a cotton bud (Q-tip) in water and place this in their enclosure. Your spider will go and drink from it when thirsty and it is amazing how they know how to do this.

If you want to interact with your spider then every now and then you could hold the stick end and hold it out to your spider and they may grab the cotton ball end with their front legs and drink from it whilst you hold it. If you have a shy spider then you shouldn't do this every time because you may find they don't want to drink with you around and therefore they may become dehydrated however doing it every now and then until your spider trusts you means that when they are elderly or sick you will be able to help them more.

Cotton wool balls and sponges soaked in water are also a good way to give your spider a drink and have the added bonus of keeping humidity levels up.

Tap water is fine for your Jumping Spider but if you are worried that the tap water in your area isn't of very good quality then bottled or distilled water is fine, as long as it is plain, still water and not fizzy or flavoured. As of writing this book there has been no evidence that suggests that distilled or bottled water affects a Jumping Spiders health.

What To Avoid

I have a lot of people ask if the water for crickets and mealworms is a suitable water source for Jumping Spiders. It seems like a perfect solution as it claims to be 'drown free' however, don't buy this for your Jumpers; a spider eats and drinks by sucking up liquid and their venom dissolves their prey to a liquid texture but the gels aren't liquid enough for your spider and will clog up their mouth parts.

Another thing to avoid is standing water, you may see a lot of people saying they use bottle caps to give their spider a drink but this method is meant to be for Tarantulas NOT tiny little Jumping Spiders.

Personally, I don't recommend any standing water but some people do say they have had success with their bigger Jumping Spiders by using shallow shells without a lip to climb over so their Jumper can walk to the edge and drink easily without falling in. If it is very shallow and the spider isn't a spiderling, then it may be safe but any amount of water can be dangerous for a Jumping Spider and I would always use with caution because once they get older they start to lose their grip and they may end up falling into the water.

Chapter 8: Molting

You will not be able to control where your Jumping Spider builds their nests. I've seen people destroy their spider's sleeping sacs constantly to encourage them to nest elsewhere and whilst this can work, as they will often decide that it is easier to build their sleep sacs elsewhere than have to re-build their bed every time you disturb it, I think this is unnecessarily cruel unless they constantly build their nest by the opening of the enclosure and there is nothing else you can do. Really we should learn about the Jumping Spider and their habits (as you are doing now by reading this book) and accommodate them as much as we can rather than expecting them to conform to our preferences; after all they didn't ask to be taken is as pets.

Mostly they will always nest at the top of their enclosure in a corner and you can encourage this by putting branches/plants high up for them to climb on. Others like to feel enclosed and will hide inside tubes, flower petals or any tiny hole they can find. Again, put something like a cardboard tube higher up in the enclosure to encourage this, as you can make sure it is out of your way for opening and closing the enclosure.

Having a side opening on your enclosure or placing your enclosure upside down so you can open it from the bottom will mean you can access your Jumping Spider's home easily to feed and mist without disturbing them. Whilst it isn't too big a deal if you disturb a normal web, it can have catastrophic results if you disturb a molt.

Signs Of Molt
If food is plentiful then your Jumping Spider will most likely molt every 3-4 weeks. They will have around 5-6 molts before they are an adult.

The main sign that your spider is molting is if they are refusing feeder insects that they would normally eat yet their abdomen isn't shrinking from lack of food and they build a thick white nest and hide themselves away. They can stay in this nest anywhere up to two weeks before molting.

If you see your spider poking their head out then you can feed them a fly or moth but most of the time they don't bother eating. Shedding their exoskeleton will restrict movement and has been compared to us trying to eat with a mask over our faces. Whilst it can be worrying they can go a month without eating so it is better for them if you just remove all prey from their enclosures and leave them alone other than misting and making sure the temperature and humidity levels are kept correctly.

If you suspect that your spider has made a molt sac then you shouldn't need to feed or water them if they are holed up so if they do end up building their molt sac near the door then rather than opening the enclosure and risk breaking the sac I recommend that you simply mist through the vent holes away from your spider.

What Is Molting?
Instead of an internal skeleton like us humans have, a Jumping Spider has a hard outer shell with connecting joints known as an exoskeleton. This outer support structure helps to prevent the spider from drying out and it is extremely strong. The joints are flexible so the spider can move yet it cannot grow bigger in the way that we do.

For a spider to grow it needs to have a bigger exoskeleton, which means shedding its older one, rather like how a snake sheds it's skin, and this is the phenomenon we call molting.

Most Jumping Spiders will make a thick egg sac but if they can't spin a web for whatever reason they may molt out in the open. Watching your spider molt can be a bit disturbing if you haven't seen it before, especially if you're not expecting it as the top part of their bodies (probably what most of us would refer to as their head) literally pops off and the spider will start to wiggle their legs about to get out, very slowly. Eventually you will be left with what looks like two spiders but one is the actual spider and the other is the exoskeleton that it has shed. Some keepers have actually thought that a spider has broken into their pet's enclosure and is attacking it until they realize that what they are in fact witnessing is the spider molting!

There isn't actually any cause for concern however because they have a new exoskeleton underneath. One thing to be aware of however is that this fresh exoskeleton will be soft and it can take anywhere between a few hours and a day to harden up. In the first day or two after a molt therefore you should only give it food that can't bite or do any damage such as small flies and/or moths.

I would also avoid handling your Jumping Spider for a few days after a molt too just to be on the safe side as you could accidentally hurt them.

Age
Molting can take quite a while from start to finish and this is usually dependent upon age; younger spiders tend to molt quicker yet more frequently whereas older spiders usually go longer between molts but stay in their molt sac for longer.

For example, a young spider may molt every two weeks but will only stay in their molt sac for one or two days whereas an older spider may go for three months without molting but then stay holed up for two or three weeks. However there is no hard and fast rule and every spider is different.

It can be concerning if your spider goes a long time before molting, especially if you've had them since they were a juvenile and you are used to them shedding every few weeks. As long as your spider is eating well then you shouldn't really worry. One issue I do find with people who are new to keeping these creatures as pets is that they say that their spider hasn't molted and then it transpires that they are still feeding fruit flies to their sub-adult Jumper. Really, once a Jumping Spider has reached a certain size it needs to be eating bigger prey.

What Else Can Affect Molting?
Molting does appear to be dependent upon how often they eat; the more food they eat the sooner they molt. Often new keepers think this is good and they will brag about how their Jumping Spider eats lots and lots and then molts twice within a fortnight however although this may seem impressive it is actually thought to shorten their life span as, in effect, it is aging them quicker.

Molting also appears to be affected by temperature; the warmer the enclosure the more the spider molts, whereas if they are cold they tend to molt less frequently so if your Jumping Spider hasn't molted for a while or if you have had them for a month or so without seeing a molt it might be worth increasing the temperature.

It is also thought that molting could be affected by genetics and even being around other molting spiders but I have yet to see actual proof for this claim.

One thing that we do find with molting that is often strange and hasn't yet been explained is that some spiders from the same egg sacs will molt at different rates. Now if you had two Jumping Spiders which you separated and sent to different keepers then this could be explained by each keeper maybe having slightly different husbandry techniques, for instance, one could feed more or could keep their temperatures slightly higher than the other keeper. However, sometimes one keeper will separate their spiders and find that a few of them molt frequently and become adults yet some of their brothers and sisters are still juveniles.

Risks
Whilst it is natural and there's nothing you can do to prevent it, it can be a dangerous process.

Firstly, without a hard exoskeleton a Jumping Spider is more vulnerable to an attack, which is why they hide themselves away in a thick sac whilst they are molting. Of course in their enclosures you can keep them safe from any attacks by keeping only one spider per enclosure and clearing out any food that hasn't been eaten and if you have substrate thoroughly checking that mealworms, Dubia Roaches or other feeders haven't hidden themselves away.

Only feeding flies and moths for a few days after a molt and avoiding handling can also mean your Jumping Spider isn't put at unnecessary risk whilst their exoskeleton is hardening.

Some spiders may experience difficulty when shedding their exoskeleton and some spiders lose a limb or even suffocate during the molting process but because of their small size you can't physically help them otherwise you risk damaging them even more. The most you can do to help them is to mist more and increase the humidity in their enclosure as this extra moisture can help their skin shed easier.

If you notice your spider has lost a limb during the molting process you shouldn't worry too much as they can still successfully hunt and will more often than not grow it back on their next molt, assuming they aren't adults who have just had their final molt.

A Reminder About Humidity
You will hear a lot of conflicting advice; keep your spider dry when molting versus keep your spider wet theories. Keep in mind that anything that 'sheds it's skin' needs humidity and too dry an atmosphere can lead to a bad molt. This is why you often see spiders in pet stores with missing limbs.

My advice is to always keep humidity levels above 50% at all times and to raise this during molting periods to around 57-60%. If you do notice your spider appears to have bits of skin stuck to it after a molt then you could moisten a cotton bud (Q-tip) and gently touch it to the stuck part to soften it up.

Chapter 9: Handling

The first thing to remember is that these creatures are at heart wild animals even if you have purchased one that is captive bred. They are always going to prefer to have space to roam by themselves rather than be sat on your hand and I never recommend handling them constantly.

However, writing a book about keeping these creatures as pets I am aware that a lot of people will want to handle their spiders and so it wouldn't make sense to leave this chapter out.

Firstly, the most important advice I can give you is to be patient. Building a bond with these creatures takes time. Wait for a time when your Jumping Spider is roaming around its enclosure and then try to interact with them.

I wouldn't recommend taking them out immediately after you first get them, instead observe them and then when they are out and about in their enclosure put your hand inside and see if they will jump onto your fingers. If they do, this is great but if not then pull your hand out and leave them be.

If your spider is coming out regularly for water and to hunt and is eating well then these are usually signs that it has settled into its home so if it is still refusing to interact with you then you could maybe try hand feeding it.

To hand feed, select a prey item and gently hold it between your fingers. If you find this a bit yucky then you can use tweezers. If your spider doesn't show an interest then you could try to move the prey towards them. If the prey isn't moving then try gently wiggling your fingers or the tweezers to make it look like it is as it is the movement that attracts a Jumping Spider to its food. Your Jumping Spider may move around the prey and your hand, checking it out but eventually it should pounce and start to eat. This is when you can let go.

If your spider doesn't eat when you are hand feeding don't worry, not all of them will take food this way so don't be disheartened.

Just remove your hand/tweezers and try again another day. Some spiders will eventually start to engage with you, others won't; you may have to accept that your new pet is an observation one only, kind of like a goldfish.

It is important that your spider is not either in pre-molt or just out of a molt when you try to handle. If it is in pre-molt then handling can cause stress, which in turn can cause a difficult molt. Leave any spiders that are in pre-molt alone.

If your spider has just finished molting then you will need to leave it be for a few days so that its exoskeleton has chance to harden up otherwise you could cause serious damage or even death.

Once your spider starts to jump on your hand or take food that you offer with your fingers or tweezers then the next step is to take it out of its enclosure completely. This is risky as they can be super quick and a lot of owners have lost Jumping Spiders this way, especially when they are new to handling such tiny spiders as these.

If you are going to take your Jumping Spider out then you should move their enclosure to an area that is free from clutter or tidy up a large space around the enclosure. These creatures like to be high up so it is a good idea to place the enclosure on top of an empty table rather than on the carpet.

If you have never handled a Jumping Spider before then I would recommend that you simply place it in another container such as a Tupperware box with the lid off. They will still be able to jump out but at least you have them in a contained area while you try to interact with them.

Make sure you take any other pets out of the room so that they don't harm your spider. If it is the first time handling then I would also make sure that it's just you in the room rather than having lots of people. I also wouldn't recommend having young children around either until you are used to handling your Jumping Spider and are are better at anticipating their movements and speed because if your spider – or child - gets spooked then your new pet could get seriously injured.

Don't grab your spider to get it out of the enclosure; it needs to get used to you so use a small, soft paintbrush, straw or an index card or similar to gently guide the spider to the opening and outside of the enclosure. Only do this if your spider was wandering about anyway; if it is resting in its sac then leave it be.

Once your Jumping Spider is out of its enclosure give it time to get used to its new surroundings rather than expecting it to jump straight onto your hand. If your spider has been interacting with you previously such as allowing you to hand feed or touching your hand with its legs when you are opening and closing it's enclosure then it may well jump straight on but if not let it get used to being out and just observe it's movements.

To give your spider something to do and make it feel more secure you could have a large plant on the table for them to climb and sit on or have cardboard tubes for them to hide in. If you line up some cardboard tubes or plastic bottles your spider may jump from one to another, which can be great fun to watch.

If your spider does handfeed then you could have some food ready to feed them or if you are using the Tupperware container idea above then you could place a mealworm or other none flying prey in there for your spider to eat. Just remember that as the lid won't be on the tub you don't want to use flies or crickets or anything else that can fly or jump away easily.

I recommend keeping a cup or small plastic tub or container handy to catch your spider in should it look like it's going to fall or try to escape.

If you leave your enclosure open then your Jumping Spider may try to just run back inside where it feels safe. If you want your spider to stay out there you should close the enclosure back up so that it can't return until you decide to put it back.

Your Jumping Spider may still return to its enclosure but if it starts exploring then this is a sign that it is comfortable and not stressed. Signs that your spider is exploring its surroundings are;

- Moving slowly with no sudden movements.
- If it stops waving it's front legs around to feel the air.
- Finding a comfortable spot and cleaning itself.

Once your spider is exploring its surroundings and seems happy and content then you can try to handle it. You could either put your hand out – palm facing upwards – directly in front of the sider and gently nudge it's abdomen with a paintbrush, small card or straw to guide it towards your hand. Watch its reaction carefully as it may allow you to guide it on but then jump straight back off again.

Another way to get your spider onto your hand is to try and trick it. Wait until your spider is at the highest spot it can get to – this might be the top of a pot plant or a tall tube or at the edge of the table. Place your hand at the same height of the spider but about three centimetres (approximately one inch) away; this should trigger it to jump if it is interested.

Sometimes what you will find is that it will jump and immediately change its mind and leap away again either back to where it started or in a different direction altogether. As long as it's safe you should be able to just let it jump but if you think it might get hurt then be ready with your catching cup.

Be patient and if your spider does leap away immediately then just keep repeating this sequence – taking it out of enclosure, letting it climb then putting your hand out for it to jump on – on a regular basis until your spider feels comfortable enough to stay.

Once your spider is sat on one hand you can put your other hand up and spaced slightly apart for it to jump on that one.

Jumping Spiders like light and heat so you could put a small desk lamp out on your table for it to sit on. Some friendlier ones may happily sit on TV or computer screens because of the heat and light they emit.

If your Jumping Spider doesn't appear to like the feel of your skin then you could wear gloves when handling – either rubber gloves like the type used for washing up or the plastic surgical type ones or possibly even cotton ones used for gardening. Just remember to only use these for handling; you don't want to use gloves that you wear for bleaching to handle your spider just in case there are chemical residues there.

Another thing to avoid is using any soap or hand cream that may contain essential oils as these can poison your Jumping Spider. Ideally if you are handling without gloves then your hands need to be completely clean and free from products. It is thought that if you smoke this can also affect your Jumping Spiders as it leaves toxins on your skin that although aren't harmful to us can be very dangerous to them.

Your Jumping Spider may be very skittish when you first take it out of its enclosure and try to handle it. After a few minutes it should calm down but, just like a dog or a cat, their personalities vary; some are friendlier and calmer than others. Hyllus Diardi and Phidippus Regius tend to be people friendly whereas the Phidippus Audax and the Phidippus Johnsoni varieties appear to be jumpy at first but become tame fairly quickly.

The more you repeat these handling techniques the less time it should take for your spider to calm down but if you do have one that is constantly jumping and never settled then you may have to make the decision not to handle it because it might not be worth stressing it out. Some spiders just don't want to interact, especially those that are slightly older or wild caught; please don't have a Jumping Spider as a pet purely so that you can interact. If they are not keen on handling then it is not important; they're not like dogs and cats that thrive on cuddles and petting. Indeed not handling is more likely to reduce their stress levels and therefore lead to a longer and more fulfilling life for these creatures. Respect their boundaries and form a bond and trust from afar.

I've known Jumping Spiders that have been captive bred yet never wanted to interact then when they've become adults they've suddenly jumped onto my hand out of the blue when I'm cleaning out food debris from their enclosures. I believe this is because they have taken time to get used to me and have decided I am not a threat. This shows that they are comfortable and it is an incredible feeling when this happens so don't give up on your Jumping Spider.

It is far more important to build a trusting relationship than to handle every day. I believe these creatures are incredibly intelligent and they appear to know when they need help and if they trust their owner they often allow them to do this, for instance, there are lots of stories of Jumping Spiders that have had a bad molt or got their leg caught in webbing allowing their owners to help.

Lost Spiders

Sometimes you may lose a Jumping Spider either because you were handling it and they ran away or because they escaped through a small hole in their tank; this is especially common for babies.

So how do you find an escapee, especially a tiny one?

Firstly look up high, as mentioned previously they like to climb so look around the room at the highest spots as they may have decided to make a nest in a corner or be hunting on the ceiling.

If you have any plants in the room that they were last seen in then check these as your Jumping Spider may have decided that this is a nice spot to make their new home. Check all the leaves and the soil at the bottom of the plant.

Remember that Jumping Spiders also like heat and light so check around door and window frames. Look for any bright, warm spots or sunbeams shining through the window as your Jumping Spider may be attracted by these. If they went missing in a room with a television or computer then check the screens as if it they were on your spider may be enticed by the heat and warmth of these electronics.

If there is still no sign of your Jumping Spider then turn all the lights off and shine a spot on the ceiling – either with a desk lamp or a torch – near to their enclosure.

Next leave out a container with some food in; the lid will need to be off in order for your spider to get it so mealworms or food that doesn't fly or jump is the best.

You could also leave a cotton bud (Q tip) sweetened with orange juice or diluted honey as they may decide to come and drink especially if they are used to taking water this way.

Remember Jumping Spiders like to hide so check behind picture frames or any other nook and crannies.

It can be sad if you lose a Jumping Spider that you class as a pet but often they do turn up so don't lose hope.

Chapter 10: Common Medical Conditions

Okay, I'm not saying your Jumping Spider is going to come down with an illness like a cold or sickness bug like some other pets might but there are some common conditions that can affect Jumping Spiders and this section is to help you identify those and offer help wherever possible although because Jumping Spiders are so small by the time you have noticed an issue it may be too late.

Heatstroke
Just like in people, heatstroke is caused by overheating and often occurs when a Jumping Spider's enclosure has been placed in direct sunlight and either the enclosure has heated up and not cooled down quickly enough or the spider hasn't had enough shelter inside their enclosure to be able to get some shade.

Treatment
Firstly, move the enclosure out of direct sunlight immediately, mist your spider's container and make sure their habitat is warm but NOT hot and offer a cotton bud (Q-tip) soaked in water.

If you are able to stay in the room with them then it may be an idea to take them out of the enclosure that is too hot and move them to either cooler temporary accommodation with a lid or put them in a Tupperware container with the lid off and a bit of food and water.

Sadly, most Jumping Spiders don't survive heatstroke.

Egg Binding
This is when a female Jumping Spider is unable to lay her eggs or the eggs have formed inside. It is common in reptiles and birds but not much has been documented about this problem in Jumping Spiders, possibly because they have only become popular as pets in recent years or possibly because keepers don't recognise that their spiders have become egg bound and therefore don't document it.

There may be some kind of discharge, which indicates an infection and if you notice this you could possibly take your spider to a vet that specializes in exotic pets if you have one although this is probably a long shot. As not enough is known about it, there is no known cure or treatment and it appears that once a Jumping Spider is egg bound she will most often die.

Mismolt
This is when a Jumping Spider is unable to properly shed its exoskeleton. As mentioned earlier there is very little you can physically do to help them partly because they are so small and partly because their new exoskeleton is so soft that any attempt at helping them could result in death or serious damage.

Anyone who is familiar with keeping reptiles as pets will know that when they struggle to shed their skin the best way to help is to provide extra humidity and this is probably the best way to help a Jumping Spider too. The extra moisture can help them shed easier so I would always recommend that you mist more often whenever you suspect that your spider is molting rather than waiting until they are struggling.

Mis-molt doesn't always end in death but usually loss of limbs and Jumping Spiders do appear to be able to hunt and live their lives as normal; there have been Jumping Spiders found in the wild with as little as three legs in total.

As long as the mis-molt wasn't their final molt then they can regrow their limbs the next time round so if you are worried I would use feeders such as flies and moths that can't hurt your spider and feed other insects such as mealworms and roaches using your fingers or tweezers until their next molt.

Drowning
It is very common with spiderlings, as they are so small that even a small droplet of water can trap them.

If you catch the Jumping Spider in time and manage to gently get it out of the water you should place it on a piece of kitchen roll/paper towel as this can absorb the water.

The best way to avoid drowning is to mist with a water bottle that has a very fine mist and always provide drinking water in the form of a wet paper towel or a cotton bud (Q-tip) soaked in water rather than using drippers, large droplets or bottle caps full of water.

Passive Recessive Disorder

This is common in Phidippus Regius (Regal Jumping Spiders) and although the actual causes are unknown it is thought to be a genetic condition.

Those that are suffering from this disorder turn white in colour and may have both male and female characteristics as well as exhibiting unusual behavior that may mean they need to be hand fed rather than left to hunt by themselves.

If they do survive long enough to reach adulthood they usually die during or shortly after their last molt.

Dehydration

Jumping Spiders can go a long time without food and be fine but they do get dehydrated very quickly especially when they are kept as pets where humidity is often lower and water access limited as opposed to when they live in the wild and have regular rainfall to drink.

The best way to prevent your spider from becoming dehydrated is to make sure there is enough humidity in their enclosure as well as putting in either a paper towel soaked in water or a wet cotton bud (Q tip) or two for them to drink from and to change these on a daily basis.

Blocked Spindles

Sometimes a Jumping Spider's spindles will seize up or become blocked which makes them unable to make any webbing. This means they won't be able to build a sleeping or molting sac nor will they be able to spin a 'drag line' to catch themselves when hunting and climbing.

If you notice your spider trying to make a nest but unable to then you could try to unblock their spindles by increasing heat and light a little although keep an eye on your spider and don't make it too hot or too light as this can cause other health issues.

Again, mist more often and put in more cotton swabs and/or kitchen roll or paper towels soaked in water as you may notice the spider trying to soak their spindles as this can help. Again, don't overdo it and always keep an eye on your spider as you don't want to drown them.

Usually their spindles become blocked after a bad molt so it is often a good idea to try and save some of their old molt sacs if you remove them when cleaning because if this does ever happen you can put it back into their enclosure so at least they have somewhere to nest until they can make webbing again.

Parasites/Mites
If you have found your Jumping Spider in the wild or have inadvertently purchased a wild caught spider then you may discover they have mites or parasites. These spiders are so tiny that you may not see any visible ones but if you do then gently try to tweezer them off, being careful not to damage your spider. Also check the enclosure and again remove any that you see with tweezers.

Mites like humid environments so lowering the humidity should kill all but those living on the spider host but of course you will need to be careful, as you don't want your spider drying out.

Usually mites and parasites and their larvae will come away with a molt so once your spider has molted make sure you remove this immediately. However, you will still need to clean your enclosure on a daily basis until you are sure they are gone.

Wash your hands with fragrance free soap/hand wash before and after cleaning and remove any substrate or decorations that could be harboring mites and either thoroughly clean or throw out and replace these. I would always recommend just using a paper towel at the bottom of the enclosure and cardboard tubes that can be removed and replaced each day until you are certain the mites have been eradicated.

Always make sure you keep any other Jumping Spiders or invertebrates or other pets away from your spider and its enclosure if you suspect it has mites or parasites as they can easily be passed on and cause health issues to other pets.

Food Stuck In Fangs

Occasionally, tough food such as a cricket exoskeleton can become stuck in your Jumping Spiders fangs.

Again, the general advice for anything that is stuck is to raise the temperature and mist more so that your enclosure becomes more humid.

Get a wet cotton bud (Q-tip) and gently touch where the fangs are stuck in the prey every now and then as this could soften it, similar to how you would soak dishes to get rid of stuck food. You could also leave a few cotton swabs lying around in the enclosure as the spider may attempt to hydrate itself.

As a last resort you could very gently try tweezers if the Jumping Spider is an adult but I would only recommend if the food is hanging out so that you can gently pull at the food with the tweezers and not the spider's mouth parts but this is very dangerous as you could do more damage than good.

Isoflourane is a gas anaesthetic that is used on tarantulas and other inverts safely and a few people have recommended this in the past but of course this would only be available via an exotic pet vet and not all vets have access or are willing to treat Jumping Spiders so I probably wouldn't even bother enquiring. Plus, I cannot comment for certain as to whether it would adversely affect a Jumping Spider or not; these spiders are so tiny that you could end up giving them far too high a dose.

Dyskinetic Syndrome (DKS)

This is a phrase that was coined by an amateur tarantula keeper and at the time of writing there has been no scientific research to back this up. If I'm honest I am inclined to believe that this isn't an actual disease but rather a bunch of symptoms that could point to a number of other causes however, it is worth noting in this book because it is something you will come across if you do more research and also because it is worth knowing various symptoms your spider could display even if you don't know the actual cause.

The main symptoms associated with DKS is poor co-ordination, a loss of appetite and a jerking, almost seizure like movement and sadly there is no known cure.

Some spider keepers have put forward a theory that these symptoms could be caused by pesticides either from wild caught insects that have been fed to the Jumping Spiders or things that are present in the air such as pollen, airborne chemicals, essential oils, flea treatments used for cats and dogs or even infections that may be passed on from humans when handling. It would therefore be wise not use essential oils or flea treatment in the same room as your Jumping Spider and to keep other pets away from them as well.

Also always wash your hands before handling or you could even wear gloves to prevent anything harmful on your skin being picked up by your Jumping Spider.

Treatments
Sadly for pretty much all of the conditions listed above there is no known cure, therefore with these types of pets prevention really is better than cure and keeping them healthy is about making sure they live in the optimum conditions.

Unlike a more common pet like a hamster you can't really take your Jumping Spider to a vet when they display symptoms. You may have an exotic vet nearby but my experience is that most don't tend to deal with Jumping Spiders and to be honest by the time you notice a problem it is often too late anyway.

If you are worried about your Jumping Spider then I would always recommend joining social media groups and asking for advice and listening to other, more experienced keepers, even then it is often guess work.

There are a few things that are commonly recommended by keepers whenever a Jumping Spider has an issue. First is to raise the humidity levels by misting more. Second is to provide them with something sweet like sugar water, orange juice or honey water. If using raw honey then this can have antibacterial properties as well. The best way to administer any of this is on a cotton bud (Q-tip) and hover it in front of your spider, hopefully they will take notice and drink from it. A very sick spider may ignore it, in which case just leave the cotton swab in the enclosure and maybe return later and try again.

If your Jumping Spider is too weak to hunt then you should also try to feed them either a crushed cricket or a fly that has been de-winged. You could hand feed or hold the prey with tweezers so that the spider can eat without having to use too much energy. If your spider is in its resting sac but near the entrance to this then just hold or place the food at this doorway and eventually your Jumping Spider will take it if it is hungry.

Euthanasia
A Jumping Spider that is dying falls into the position known as the 'death curl' where their legs start to curl up underneath them.

This isn't something I recommend lightly and it is a widely debated argument, which people have very strong opinions on whichever side they are on.

My thoughts on euthanasia is that if your Jumping Spider is suffering then it is often the most humane action although should only be a final resort if you have tried the other things recommended above.

Most of us don't have access to a gas anaesthetic so unless you have a vet that is willing to euthanise your spider for you then the best way to do it at home is to put your spider in the fridge to dull it's senses and then place it in the freezer which will kill it.

Your second option is blunt trauma, which in essence means quickly squashing the spider. This is a quicker death for your spider (and for you) but of course I realise that most people won't want to squash their beloved pets.

Chapter 11: Breeding

Responsible Breeding

There are many reasons why somebody would want to breed their pets. Often it is just another facet of their hobby. which they do for experience or for the pleasure of raising a pet from a baby through to an adult or sometimes it is done to try and make money from the offspring.

Whatever your reasons for breeding your Jumping Spiders it shouldn't be a decision you make lightly. Unlike breeding a cat or dog that may result in a birth of a few babies at most, Jumping Spiders can leave you with three hundred plus babies to look after. Whilst it may be fun for you, please remember that these are living creatures and I don't believe in breeding only to kill the offspring afterwards because you realize you have too many to cope with.

If you have found your pet in the wild then there is no reason why you can't release the offspring back outside once the weather is warm enough for them to survive but if you live in a country where the Jumping Spider you have is not a native one then you cannot release them back out into the wild because they are an invasive species and can have adverse effects on the environment, assuming they survive at all. For example, there are no Jumping Spiders in England out in the wild so it would be very irresponsible for you to release your Jumping Spiderlings into your back garden or nearby woodland.

Not all spiderlings survive and even the most experienced breeders tend to lose some but you could still end up with hundreds; how realistic is it for you to care for and/or re-home this many Jumping Spiders?

As for money, you need to keep these babies until they are old enough to be transported safely. Some people do make money from selling Jumping Spiders but I would recommend you sit and work out whether it is worth it before you go ahead and breed your spider pets. For example, you may have two hundred spiders but by the time they are old enough to leave you there may only be forty or fifty left. That means you're only making money from a quarter of them yet you could have been feeding over a hundred, three or four fruit flies each per day, for a month or more. Add in shipping costs and this could end up costing you more than you actually sell the spiders for and that's assuming you find buyers in the first place; most people do prefer to buy from an established breeder rather than a novice. Also, you need to consider what you would do if somebody buys a spider from you but then complains that it was dead on arrival; if you reimburse then you are losing money.

One reason some keepers have given for breeding is because their female spider lays infertile clutches and they 'felt bad' about taking away these eggs. This is a ridiculous reason for breeding because of course these people then ended up with hundreds of babies, which they struggled to re-home. A female Jumping Spider that lays infertile eggs often knows when they are infertile and whilst she may be stressed if you tried to take them away once she leaves abandons them of her own accord it seems to have no adverse effect.

If you do decide you want to breed your Jumping Spiders then I would recommend you only do so after you have had experience of successfully keeping these creatures over a long period of time, preferably a few years or more as taking care of spiderlings is a huge challenge. Don't get in over your head by breeding and then realising that you can't take care of them.

Mating
Putting a male and female Jumping Spider together can often have very different results depending on the spiders.

You can either put your male into your female Jumping Spider's enclosure or you can use a completely different container so they are on neutral territory. If you do use a different enclosure to breed then put the female in first so she can get used to the new area before you introduce your male.

Before you put your male and female together make sure you feed your female well beforehand otherwise she will just eat the male spider. Once they are in the same enclosure together make sure you put in extra flies and crickets as well so they don't fight over food.

Even well fed and with the extra food there is always the risk that your female spider will eat the male, sometimes before they have even mated, sometimes afterwards so always keep an eye on your spiders when they are together, don't keep them together for more than a few days, preferably less and always separate after mating has taken place.

If you have captured a Jumping Spider from outside then you should be aware that females can store sperm for up to a year. In the wild Jumping Spiders tend to pair up in the autumn/fall but the female will store sperm over winter whilst the eggs are developing. When they are ready to be laid the eggs will pass over the sperm, which is how they are fertilized. Therefore your new pet may already be gravid. If this is the case she won't mate with any male that you put in her enclosure and will most likely just attack and kill him instead. It therefore would be wise to not breed a wild caught female but if you do you should wait a few months first to see if she makes an egg sac otherwise you risk losing your male very quickly.

One more point to make is that even if you buy your spiders in the UK they could still have been wild caught then shipped to you so make sure that you buy from a breeder and check that they breed the spiders themselves. I would always ask for photographs of their adult spider's and spiderlings enclosures so you can be certain that this is the case.

Mating season in the wild tends to be August to October but in captivity this may deviate slightly as their days and nights will be dictated by your routines as opposed to the natural day and night cycles they would experience in the great outdoors.

When you are ready to breed your Jumping Spiders it is important that they are both fully grown adults, otherwise breeding won't take place, not only that but again they could just fight and end up with one of them being killed.

I also wouldn't recommend you try to mate an older female with a younger male; not only will the eggs most likely be infertile anyway but if she decides she doesn't want to mate she may get aggressive or if she is slower due to age the male may end up killing her in self-defense.

When you first introduce your spiders it is important that you do so at a time when you can watch them in case your female isn't receptive to breeding.

Females are bigger than males and are the more dominant; whether the two mate will be entirely up to your female. This is an advantage of using a Tupperware container or something similar, as you can leave the lid off until you are certain that your spiders are getting along. Of course you won't be able to put in any food that can fly or jump out and the downside to this is that your spiders may try to escape rather than breed so my advice is to keep either a small, soft paint brush or some small credit card sized pieces of cardboard or index cards next to the container which you can use to usher your spiders back should they try to run away or to separate them if they start to fight.

Usually the male will start to 'dance' and there will be a lot of abdomen wiggling and forearm waving as well as vibrations, which some scientists describe as 'singing' or 'serenading'.

Your male may do his 'courtship dance' but may be cautious; often they will stay out of the female's direct eye line. Whatever you do, don't push the male towards the female however, otherwise he will most likely get eaten.

Watch your female closely; she may appear disinterested and ignore the male despite his best efforts, even turning away, but this can be a good sign.

If she looks aggressive however and puts her front legs up in a defensive pose then I would get ready to separate the two as this could be a sign that she is going to pounce and attack him.

Some female species of Jumping Spider's will attack the male yet the male will persist and eventually the two will mate. However, I would always separate if you see any sign that your female is going to attack and try again another day. You can't rush the breeding process otherwise you risk losing your male. With these creatures it can take a lot of time and patience.

If the female is agreeable and decides to accept your male then she will move into a more passive position and allow the male to get close to her. Once this has happened it is safe to leave the two of them alone so if they are in a lidless container you can add a fly or two and put the lid on and leave them to it.

Keep checking on the two of them and remove once you are certain that the two have mated.

How To Know If Successful

Female spiders don't have live births like dogs and cats do but rather they are an egg laying species and therefore don't get 'pregnant' as such but they could still display similar symptoms.

For instance, the female's abdomen may become larger and look like it may explode which is the main symptom that she is gravid and about to lay eggs. If you notice this then you should consider making your enclosure spiderling safe or placing your female in a different container (See Below).

Next, your female spider may start to build an elaborate silk hammock which she will hide inside and then she will eventually lay her eggs into an egg sac made of silk thread.

The final symptom is that she refuses to eat or drink.

Preparing For Spiderlings

If you have mated your females or suspect she is gravid – as mentioned previously wild caught females may have mated before you found them – then you should 'baby' proof your enclosure.

I cannot stress enough how tiny these spiderlings can be and when they disperse from the sac they can quickly escape. Basically, if you have any holes or gaps that are larger than half a grain of rice then your enclosure isn't secure! You may end up with hundreds of spiderlings too and may not even notice that any have escaped until it is too late! I will point out here that a Jumping Spider – depending on species – can have laid between two to one thousand eggs at any one time! Thankfully, most of the Jumping Spiders kept as pets don't seem to have as many as these but even so many owners have been left with a couple hundred eggs.

If you can't make your current spider enclosure secure or are worried about it then you have two choices; you can either move the mother into a secure enclosure BEFORE she lays eggs OR you can place the whole of your current enclosure into a butterfly net. Just be aware that once the mother has laid the eggs then it is too late to move her.

If you are going to move your female into a new enclosure until her eggs have hatched then many people successfully use a plastic deli cup with tiny air holes poked into it. Turn the deli cup upside down so you can open and close it easily when you need to. Put a small hole in which you can put in food when the slings have hatched then cover this hole with duct tape. Don't worry, the mother and her spiderlings will not stick to the duct tape. When they have hatched and you need to feed your new babies you can simply uncover the hole, put a funnel in it and pour fruit flies into the funnel, which prevents both your spiderlings and the fruit flies from escaping.

Egg Laying

Female Jumping Spider's that become gravid from successful mating can take anywhere between one day and two weeks plus to lay their eggs, depending on the species. The females are able to store sperm for up to a year so it could take longer and you may end up with several clutches within that year that are all fertile just from one mating.

Eggs are laid in a thick fluffy egg sac usually made at the top of their enclosures, often in a spot that they tend to favour for their sleeping sacs.

Once the eggs have been laid you may notice that your female ventures out more often but be careful as she may suddenly become aggressive as she is protecting her eggs so don't disturb the egg sac in any way otherwise you could get bitten!

Some female spiders won't leave the egg sac for many days and may even stay there until after the eggs hatch; this is normal but keep an eye on her as she may become very weak and dehydrated.

You can offer food but make sure it's flies – wingless fruit flies are ideal as they are easy to catch and eat and won't attack her or cause any damage if she stays in the egg sac. Don't offer anything that is challenging or aggressive such as crickets or roaches. If your female is uninterested you could try feeding and offering water by hand.

Put in cotton buds (Q-tips) soaked in water for her to drink.

Hatching
The eggs will take around 1-4 weeks to hatch depending on enclosure temperature and the type of Jumping Spider it is. The babies will stay inside the egg sac until they have had their first molt.

Leave the egg sac be until the slings emerge. Many Jumping Spiders develop at different rates, especially in captivity, and you may see a few slings moving about whilst others are still inside their eggs. It may look as if these ones are infertile but it could just be that they are going to hatch later.

You will still need to mist but should only use a very, very fine mist. You may find a small spritzing bottle from a drug store (kind of like an atomizer type bottle) may be preferable to using a normal spray bottle from a garden centre or hardware store.

Once the spiderlings emerge, if the droplets are too large your spiderlings could drown. Again, never spray them directly. You may find that when you spritz they run away and take cover anyway.

The mother may remain in the egg sac even after the spiderlings have emerged. Leave her be and then once she emerges you can move her back into her old enclosure. Assuming you have used the deli cup idea, if you just placed her original enclosure into a butterfly net or managed to spiderling proof it then you will need to move the mother to a new enclosure so make sure you have this ready.

Remember, she will be very weak and most likely thirsty so put in some food for her immediately as well. I would probably recommend you just give a few fruit flies or hand feed a blue or green bottle fly and give water from a cotton bud (Q-tip) or place a wet paper towel inside her enclosure and leave her be.

Sometimes the mother will die in the nest, this could be due to her age or because she has become dehydrated and weak from hunger after laying the eggs. This can be very sad when you view them as a pet. If this happens and the babies are still in the nest then just leave the mother where she is until the babies emerge, otherwise you risk accidentally injuring them if you try to remove her whilst the spiderlings are still inside as they are very fragile at this stage.

Once they emerge you will have to feed them; they will only eat small prey such as fruit flies or aphids and feeding can be challenging to say the least, as you will need to prevent both the flies and the spiderlings from escaping. This is why a funnel is recommended when feeding.

Live, moving prey is far more attractive than dead prey so even if the mother or another baby killed a fruit fly always put in more live ones for the others to eat. Rather than put in one at a time you should put in three or four fruit flies per spiderling.

You will find that they will leave the nest to feed on fruit flies and return at night to rest, this is perfectly normal.

Separating Spiderlings
A week or two after the slings have emerged you will need to start separating them, otherwise they will start to cannabilise (eat) each other. There is no exact time limit on this; some people will say it depends on the type of Jumping Spider, others will say that it will depend on the age of the spiderlings, which is why I recommend one to two weeks.

I can see the appeal for keeping the spiderlings together for as long as possible; funneling a whole bunch of fruit flies into one deli cup is a lot easier than funneling two or three into twenty plus different containers and once they have been separated feeding, watering and misting becomes incredibly time consuming. Once they start to turn on each other it really is the survival of the fittest and usually it's the smallest or the 'runts' that are the first to be eaten.

Once they are big enough to be separated, then you can feed and water (on a paper towel or cotton bud) every three days.

When the spiderlings are about half the size of a housefly you can start feeding them flies but don't feed any larger or more aggressive prey such as crickets and roaches until they are roughly the size of the prey. I.e. you can feed them pinhead crickets when the spiderlings are about the same size. Once they have reached this stage you can start to sell or adopt them out.

High mortality rates and cannabilism is perfectly normal (and indeed should be expected) with these creatures, especially when they are born into captivity where space is limited and depending on housing conditions and the species even the very best breeders can lose anywhere between 25% to 95% of their spiderlings. This is another reason why you should be fairly experienced in keeping one Jumping Spider on its own before attempting to breed; these spiders are living creatures and thus shouldn't be treated like science experiments at home.

Babies Leaving Nest Too Early

This is a fairly rare occurrence but sometimes an egg sac may not have enough silk which causes the babies to fall out before they are ready to leave. If this happens, then remove the egg sac and put some surrogate webbing over the top until the spiderlings are ready to molt. This surrogate webbing could be some old silk taken from the mother spider or from another Jumping Spider you may have – for instance, it could be just some of the silk from the drag lines or from an old sleeping or molting sac.

If you don't have any webbing then you could shred a cotton ball up, make a hole in it and place the egg sac inside this hole. This should keep the babies inside until they are fully developed.

If the babies do leave the nest before their first molt then you can use a small, soft paintbrush and gently put them back inside as best you can.

To know if a baby is ready to leave the nest then look for eyes and a mouth; if they have obvious eyes then they have molted once but if their eyes are barely visible and it looks like there is a layer of 'skin' or membrane covering them and/or if they haven't a 'developed' mouth as such then they are first instar and haven't yet molted.

How quickly your spiderlings molt will be dependent on temperature so if you are concerned that they are taking a while you could check your levels and possibly increase it if they are on the low side.

If you notice that a spiderling has left the nest but is struggling to walk and keeps flipping over onto it's back then this is a sign that it is about to molt. Again, if possible try to put it back in the nest but if not keep misting regularly and make sure your humidity levels are high enough to aid the spider's molt.

Infertile Eggs

If your Jumping Spider is a wild caught female but you had her as a pet before she was old enough to mate or she is a captive bred spider that has never been with a male she will still lay eggs but of course these won't be fertile and therefore will never hatch.

Despite this, the female will still make an egg sac and guard them for around 1-2 weeks before abandoning it. Again, you can still offer food and water but don't panic if she doesn't eat or drink in this time.

Don't disturb or remove the egg sac in anyway. You may think it is kinder to take it away rather than leave her to sit there for two weeks but actually it could cause your female unnecessary stress and make them agitated which can have a negative impact on her health.

Some females have been known to die guarding eggs and if you are worried that your female has gone longer than two weeks without eating or drinking then coax her out by gently pushing on top of the nest and guiding her towards the opening with a small paintbrush. However I only say this as a last resort as it is far better for them to come out by themselves.

I would always recommend that you keep misting and offering food. Put a fly in the freezer until it is barely moving then offer it to her at the opening to the nest so she doesn't have to come out far to eat it. She may take it from your fingers or if you leave it she may eventually take it into her nest. This is far more preferable than coaxing the female out.

Once your female has left the nest you can remove and destroy it. You need to do this otherwise it will start to grow bacteria. Your female may instinctively know that they are infertile and may lose interest after a week or so anyway.

Life Expectancy After Eggs
Research suggests that some Jumping Spiders, such as the Phidippus Apacheanus, die shortly after their spiderlings emerge. However, in captivity this isn't always true and it can be their third egg sac or more before the female passes guarding her eggs.

There could be many reasons as to why females in the wild die when guarding egg sacs, which could be eliminated in captivity. For example, in the wild the temperatures may be colder than they are in someone's house so the female spiders in the wild may die because they are guarding their eggs for longer whereas in captivity their eggs develop at a faster rate because it is warmer.

Also, in the wild the female may be weak when she eventually emerges and may struggle to find or capture food. In captivity however, there won't be as much space and their keeper will constantly keep a good supply of food in their enclosure which means that hunting is a lot easier. Plus, if the spider is weak, a keeper may in fact hand feed or put it right at the entrance to their nest which they wouldn't get in the wild.

Again, in the wild they may struggle to find water whereas in captivity they should have this supplied via regular misting plus a wet cotton ball or cotton bud (Q tip) in their enclosure.

Different species and genus have different characteristics and how long a female survives after laying eggs – fertile or not – depends on how good the husbandry techniques are and how strong and healthy the spider is as well as her age. For example, I know some people who have had Phidippus Johnsoni spiders lay one clutch then die whilst others have laid four clutches and are still alive six months later. Others have Phidippus Regius females who have laid only two clutches and are barely eating afterwards whilst some have regals who are on their fifth or sixth clutch.

I think part of the reason why it is difficult to say how many clutches a female will have or how long they will live afterwards is because there is not enough information out there. Whilst there are plenty of anecdotes on social media and a few scientific studies on various things there still needs to be more in order to give a definitive answer.

Unwanted Eggs

This is a huge issue and is why many people don't recommend that you capture an adult female unless you are interested in raising spiderlings.

There are two reasons why people end up with unwanted spider eggs; either they caught their female in the wild without knowing she had already mated or else they bred their pet spider without realising she would produce a large amount of eggs. Often people breed their pets thinking it is a money spinner then struggle to find buyers or find it difficult to look after them until they are old enough to be sold.

If you end up with unwanted eggs because you captured your female in the wild then I don't see this as an issue because she must be a native species therefore you can just release the spiderlings once they have dispersed from the egg sac. There is no negative ecological impact because if you hadn't captured her, those babies would have been born into the wild anyway.

If you do this then pick a nice area with lots of plants for them to hunt and nest in and choose a nice, cloudy morning so that they have the best chance of survival. I know some people who are real spider lovers that relocate any of their baby spiders and their mother into their garden shed so that they have warmth and shelter should they need it yet can disperse into the garden so have plenty of room to roam.

Unwanted eggs is really more of an issue in the latter scenario when the spider has been bred in captivity and the owner realizes that there are hundreds of spiderlings that they can't get rid of. If the species isn't native to the country they are living in - for example, no Jumping Spiders are native to the UK - then they shouldn't be released into the wild as this can have a negative environmental impact.

However, if you ended up with spiderlings and you cannot release them back into the wild then you may have no choice but to destroy the egg sac before they hatch. I really cannot stress enough that I am only recommending this as a last resort. It would be preferable to go onto a social media group dedicated to Jumping Spiders, explain the situation and ask somebody if they would be willing to take the babies off your hands. Sometimes somebody will offer to take if they are shipped to them.

If you really have no other choice then destroy the nest at night; put the mother spider in a separate container then either very carefully remove the eggs from the sac without destroying it or place the whole egg sac in the freezer for a few hours to kill the spiderlings, then place the egg sac back in with the mother.

Many people ask me if killing the spiderlings has a negative impact on the mother and I really can't say for sure either way. Having the egg sac intact rather than just removing it should reduce the stress and I would imagine it is then the same as when she lays an infertile clutch however, she may still appear agitated and may even refuse to eat or drink for a few weeks, if your female is older she may die but whether this is due to stress or just old age I don't think anybody could say.

Chapter 12: Aging

Age Progression

Once your spider gets to around a year old or more they may start to show signs of aging. You may find that your spider doesn't produce as much silk, eats less and struggles to climb.

Less Silk

If your spider doesn't produce as much silk then you may find that their sleep sacs aren't as thick as they once were and there will be less webbing around the enclosure. Once you suspect your spider is reaching old age it may be worthwhile saving any old sleep sacs or molt sacs so that you can put these back in should your spider struggle to make new ones.

Getting An Old Spider To Eat

It can be worrying when your spider stops eating especially if it used to have a very good appetite. Not eating can make your spider sluggish, which can also be alarming. Make sure you mist every day to ensure that the spider is getting water. If your spider is sluggish you could give them some honey water on a cotton bud (Q Tip).

If your spider is struggling to hunt you could try to handfeed them but if they don't take food from you then you could injure a bluebottle and put it as close to the spider as you can get it; if they are in a sleep sac then place it at the entrance to this.

Fruit flies don't require hunting skills so you could go back to feeding a few of those each day if your Jumping Spider has a hard time taking down bigger prey.

Spider Unable To Climb

You may find that your spider is unable to climb the walls of its tank and spends a lot of time at the bottom of its enclosure. As mentioned before, a Jumping Spider much prefers to be up high so to help try taping some material to the side of its home to help it grip for example, cross stitch aida which is material with small holes or the plastic mesh with holes, both used for cross stitching are good or you could hot glue burlap strips to the side.

Also, letting the enclosure get webbed up and not wiping the sides will also give the spider something to climb on.

Remember to watch your spider carefully as if they slip from high up they could injure themselves.

Dying

It is always sad when a pet dies and it is no different with these little guys. Just because they're spiders doesn't mean their lives have less meaning.

Sadly, Jumping Spiders don't have very long life spans even with the best of care and sometimes they can die without any apparent reason which can be even more upsetting.

A lot of people put these early, unexplained deaths down to genetics. If you do have a Jumping Spider die before it is a year old and you have kept other Jumping Spiders successfully before then chances are there would have been nothing you could do to prolong their lives.

I have heard many stories recently about Jumping Spiders in the UK being bought at pet expos, online and even in pet stores that have died after exhibiting signs of old age when the owner thought they were still juvenile or showing signs of toxin exposure and it is thought that many of these are being wild caught and shipped over to the UK and are then sold as captive bred.

A Jumping Spider that has reached old age will start to slow down and exhibit the signs listed above. Once it is dying it will slowly curl up and lay still – this is referred to as the death curl.

If your Jumping Spider has displayed signs of old age then usually there is nothing you can do for them if they are dying. If there is a little movement you could give them a cotton bud (Q tip) soaked in honey water or fruit juice and put it next to them but the best thing for them is to leave them alone rather than risk stressing them out.

Having said that, sometimes younger Jumping Spiders have started to close up into a death curl and yet have revived themselves and there are a couple of reasons that this might happen.

Firstly, they might be cold so it may be worth putting their enclosure in a warm spot near your window or leave it near a radiator or heater.

Although this is a book about keeping Jumping Spiders as pets it is worth mentioning here that if you find a Jumping Spider outside in the death curl you may believe that they haven't survived the winter yet if you bring them inside and warmed them up by a heater or in a patch of sunlight you may find they revive themselves.

Secondly, they may look like they're having a spasm then they appear to curl up so it is easy to assume that they are dying yet actually what you may have witnessed is a molt that for whatever reason they didn't make a molt sac for. Whilst this is unusual it is not unknown for them to do this either because they are getting older and are not making as much webbing or because their spindles/spinnerets have become blocked.

The third reason may be that they have been exposed to water but could dry out.

In the final two cases I would place the Jumping spider on a dry paper towel or sheet of kitchen roll and wait to see if they start moving again. The paper towel or kitchen roll will soak up any additional moisture if it is due to water. I would recommend that you take them out of their enclosure if you are going to do this just in case there is something in there that they are reacting to.

Sometimes, your Jumping Spider may get injured when you are handling; as mentioned before they are ridiculously fast and you can accidentally injure them easily either by dropping them or even unintentionally crushing them in a piece of clothing. If this happens I would put them aside and hope they recover, again give them a cotton bud (Q tip) soaked in water, honey water or orange juice and maybe even crush up an insect such as mealworm and leave this next to them. If you are lucky they will recover and molt out any injuries.

If this was your first – and only – Jumping Spider then it is worth checking your temperature and humidity levels as well as the amount of heat and light they had and other husbandry techniques just in case but sometimes there is no obvious reason.

Unfortunately, these creatures are still quite unknown and we are all still learning about them, which means that although they are living creatures and we should respect them and try to keep them as best we can, sometimes it is just a matter of trial and error. Of course in the UK you wouldn't be able to do this because they are not native creatures so the best thing to do is just learn as much about them and observe them carefully to see what works and what doesn't before purchasing.

Sometimes, death can be caused by something as innocuous as a piece of wood getting damp with misting which in turn causes mold to build up which has a negative effect on your Jumping Spider This is why I say to constantly monitor your spider and their enclosure; cleaning out regularly and checking plants and decorative items for mold, mites, parasites and so on.

For those that are breeding it is wise to separate slings by the third instar, which will give you better control over feeding and bacteria although this of course means you will have more containers to check.

Conclusion

Many people won't even consider that a spider has a personality, much less a fun, intelligent one yet Jumping Spiders do and as such make great, unique pets.

Many people will say that these spiders have helped them overcome Arachnophobia – a severe fear of spiders –but remember if you are buying one to get over your own fear that your safety and theirs is paramount and you should consider this carefully; could you realistically clean out their cage and feed them without freaking out?

If you are keeping a Jumping Spider as a pet then by all means have as many as you can cope with just don't keep them in the same enclosure. As a rule, once these creatures have reached third instar or older they need to have their own enclosure. Some owners will say that they keep their Jumping Spiders together and nothing has ever happened. To me it's not worth the risk even if you have a huge tank to keep them in, eventually one will become prey to another or even if they don't it is still possible that communal living will stress them out and shorten their life spans.

These spiders do bite but only as a defense mechanism, so handle with care. If you do get bitten and the symptoms don't seem to be improving – or indeed are getting worse –after a couple of hours or if the bite is unusually painful or swollen then it is worth getting checked out by a medical professional as a precaution, as some people can be allergic to the venom from Jumping Spiders, even if you have been bitten previously with no adverse reaction.

As a pet these creatures don't have to cost the earth and can be super cheap to house and feed. If you are in a country where Jumping Spiders live in the wild then you can, in theory, find one in your local area for free. Some people will say this is unethical because wild creatures should be left in the wild. The flip side of this however is that you may be giving the Jumping Spider an easier and longer life than it may have in the wild if you keep it in the optimum conditions. Let's face it, in the wild they are at risk of dying at a young age either by being attacked by a predator, lack of food being available or due to extreme weather conditions. Indeed, some people take in Jumping Spiders purely for the winter and release them again when the warmer months arrive.

I hope you really enjoy spending time with, and learning about, your jumping spider!

Made in the USA
Las Vegas, NV
17 December 2022

63124466R00059